P9-APR-562

Euclid Public Library
631 E. 222nd Street
Euclid, Ohio 44123
216-261-5300

150 Best of the Best Loft Ideas

150 Best of the Best Loft Ideas

HARPER
DESIGN

An Imprint of HarperCollinsPublishers

150 BEST OF THE BEST LOFT IDEAS
Copyright © 2016 by LOFT Publications

All rights reserved. No part of this book may be used or reproduced in any manner whatsoever
without written permission, except in the case of brief quotations embodied in critical articles and reviews.
For information, address Harper Design, 195 Broadway, New York, NY 10007.

HarperCollins books may be purchased for educational, business, or sales promotional use.
For information, please write the Special Markets Department at SPsales@harpercollins.com.

First published in 2016 by:
Harper Design
An Imprint of HarperCollins*Publishers*
195 Broadway
New York, NY 10007
Tel.: (212) 207-7000
Fax: (855) 746-6023
harperdesign@harpercollins.com
www.hc.com

Distributed throughout the world by:
HarperCollins*Publishers*
195 Broadway
New York, NY 10007

Editorial coordinator: Claudia Martínez Alonso
Art director: Mireia Casanovas Soley
Editor and texts: LOFT Publications
Layout: Cristina Simó Perales

ISBN 978-0-06-244452-3

Library of Congress Control Number is available upon request.

Printed in China
First printing, 2016

CONTENTS

INTRODUCTION

To discover the origin of the loft we must go back to New York in the 1950s, specifically the neighborhoods of Tribeca, SoHo, and Chelsea. In the postwar period, the US economy had undergone a transformation: goods were produced with less manpower and the number of workers in the service sector increased. In addition, large companies moved their production plants abroad, where labor was cheaper. As a result, many factories and warehouses were left empty. The need for large spaces and the high rents of apartments, together with the fact that the owners of industrial buildings were seeing their prices drop, made these unused spaces attractive to an unexpected market. Students and artists found cheap places to work and live.

These buildings lacked internal partitions. Steel structures mounted on large slabs made for spaces with generous heights. Furthermore, they were very bright, thanks to the light filtering through the huge windows of their stone façades. These were open spaces where you could grow and show all your creative activity to the full. Over time these spaces were adapted to other uses—shops, art and photography galleries. It's fair to say that, half a century later, the loft has come, more than any other space, to symbolize a modern, cutting-edge lifestyle.

The essence of the loft is an open plan, featuring visual continuity, environments that flow into one another, and copious natural light. Unified materials and color palettes, along with an absence of doors and partitions, enhance the effect. Spatial division is often achieved with slopes and changes in color, texture, or lighting. A wide range of creative solutions has been developed to replace partitions: multifunctional furniture, plants, sliding panels, glass walls...

The great ceiling height of many lofts encourages the construction of upper floors or mezzanines, which tends to separate shared areas—living room, dining room, kitchen—from bedrooms, studies, or other rooms. The staircase linking multiple levels often becomes a decorative element in and of itself.

The prevailing philosophy is to refurbish the loft, optimizing it, while retaining as many original structural elements as practicable. Beamed roofs, vaulted ceilings, columns, and ancient brickwork are all refurbished, and the pipes and ducts of the original facilities are left in plain sight, giving each space its own personal seal and style. On the other hand, made-to-measure furniture pieces are designed which, as well as exhibiting contemporary and well-polished aesthetics, often perform several roles: space separator, cupboard, display unit—the comfort and functionality of the modern harmonizes with nostalgia for the old.

Since its inception, loft style has defined itself as industrial, sober, and authentic —sometimes even cold—since it divests itself of surplus elements and any artifice. Common practice has been to use unfinished materials—cement, brick, iron, and steel—and a neutral color palette, with white predominating. But the current loft boom—including newly constructed buildings based on a nineteenth-century industrial aesthetic—has moved far beyond the "boho" with warm and welcoming spaces that retain the light and the spatial continuity of the classic loft style.

This book presents a carefully chosen and diverse selection of projects from prestigious architects around the world who, while always bearing in mind their clients' wishes, show us a series of compelling approaches to spatial design, both practical and innovative in the use of materials and light, attuned to modern and avant-garde lifestyles without neglecting aesthetic harmony and beauty. Integrated spaces, airy, light spaces in which to live and share, and, in many cases, work; in short, spaces adapted to the lives of those who inhabit them and impregnated, no doubt, with their personality.

Loft in Via Savona

Roberto Murgia

Milan, Italy

© Francesco Jodice

Four friends bought part of the first floor of an old building housing the offices of the Domus Academy, the first postgraduate design school in Italy. The clients' idea was clear: to create a space for living and working, both representative and intimate, public but private. The space was divided into four equal parts, of 1,076 square feet each, which, together with a height of nearly twenty-five feet allowed for the construction of two stories. Four identical spaces for four different inhabitants—a designer, a photographer and two directors—with similar lives, but with different souls, cultures, and dreams.

001

Carpets deliberately placed break with the uniform white, delimiting the spaces, at the same time dressing them up, providing a sense of warmth and thermal insulation.

Longitudinal section

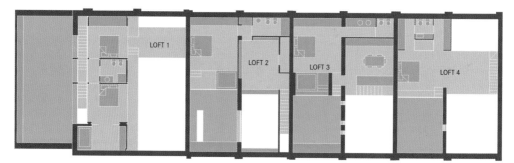

LOFT 1

LOFT 2

LOFT 3

LOFT 4

Upper-floor plan

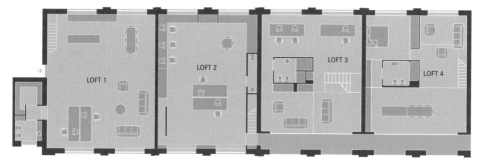

LOFT 1

LOFT 2

LOFT 3

LOFT 4

Lower-floor plan

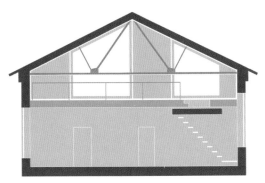

Cross section through loft 1

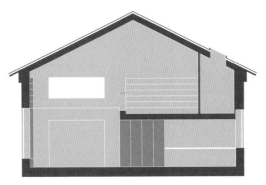

Cross section through loft 2

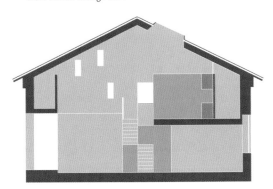

Cross section through loft 3

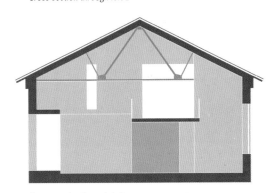

Cross section through loft 4

002

Live-work lofts make it
affordable to have office space.
Despite the openness that
generally defines lofts, living
and working functions can be
separate designated areas.

A combination of open and closed storage makes the most of the space. The wall between the deep-set windows is lined with tall open shelving, and one of the window headers allows for the display of special items. Everything else is stored in pullout cabinets, keeping the space tidy and organized.

003

Loft spaces lend to creativity, allowing the exploration of flexible and unusual configurations. This results in spaces that are unique in the expression of this creativity.

004

Staircase design has evolved from the solely functional purpose to open itself up into the creation of high-impact designs, using innovative materials and cutting-edge technology.

In addition to being a source of heat, the fireplace—like the timber-storage space, also integrated in a central wood module—becomes an important decorative component of the room.

The wood flooring brings some
warmth to the sober and austere
atmosphere created by the
predominantly white space.

005

Loft spaces highlight spatial experience, abandoning the traditional notions of domestic living, in favor of open relationships that offer direct visual connection among different zones.

006

In lieu of a solid staircase choose a trimmer and sleeker version to highlight the minimalist and open character of a space.

In the heart of Montreal, this loft, owned by an artist who collects design and art objects, pays genuine tribute to creativity. To meet the needs of the artist who wanted a home environment that would stimulate creativity, Jean Verville designed this original interior.

Combining the fun and colorful with the white and relaxing, it works to awaken the senses and blur spatial perception. The open design, along with a generous storage area, accommodates an eclectic art collection that can be continually updated and renewed.

Prismatic Colors

Jean Verville

Montreal, Canada

© Jean Verville architecte

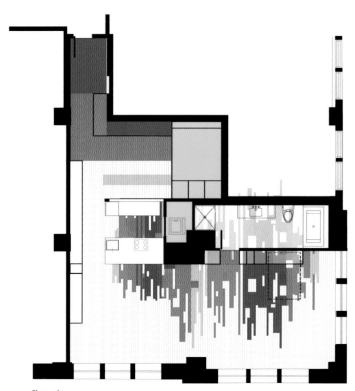

Floor plan

007

Color can be identifiers of zones. They have the power of providing a space with special qualities based on the psychological value of colors.

The floor with colored vinyl inserts is covered by a layer of bright white epoxy resin. This dwelling project is a fusion of architecture, art, and design, which cannot leave any spectator indifferent.

Amid this multicolored environment, a kitchen, in white and stainless steel, presents a clean and functional appearance. Cupboards and storage modules are used to separate the spaces.

008

Furniture can separate areas
with different functions,
while maintaining the open
feel of a space. This allows
a more flexible use of space
than walls would permit.

Whether they are white, colored, or
paneled with mirrors, the cupboards
structure this loft space.

The sleeping area, entirely in yellow, contains large storage chests camouflaged with visually impactful geometry.

House Like Village

MKA Marc Koehler Architects

Amsterdam, The Netherlands

© Marcel van der Burg

This project, involving the conversion and subdivision of a former harbor cantina into large living spaces, maintains its original open character. The interior of one of these spaces features four blocks that are conceived as houses; they contain private spaces and supporting facilities. The open areas around them are laid out as streets, which are crossed by bridges, connecting the different blocks. The rooftops of these blocks, fully functional, offer unobstructed views of the entire space, and beyond, of the walls of the container building.

009

With their flexible layout, openness, and high ceilings, loft spaces are both sophisticated and relaxed. But as attractive as this generous amount of space may be, it requires strategic organizing to equip the space with the essential commodities.

010

Not only do mezzanines and other intermediate floors between a main floor and a ceiling increase square footage but also extend visual reach, generating inviting areas.

This project was an integrated collaboration between architect, client, and contractor. Communication was critical in order to expedite the design and construction process and to meet the client's needs and expectations.

Although at first glance the space does not look kid-friendly, the home was designed with family play and the production of art in mind. Storage was also a key element of the design, fully explored throughout the loft.

Wadia Residence

Resolution: 4 Architecture

New York, New York,
United States

© Resolution: 4 Architecture

Benches below the windows add storage space without obstructing circulation. They also serve as informal seating for gatherings.

The dining area, receiving natural light
from two sides, is conveniently located
between the kitchen and the living area,
at one corner of the space.

012

Don't underestimate the
power of white in kitchens.
White amplifies the effects of
natural and artificial lighting,
which is a critical design
element in utilitarian areas.

A sculptural staircase is the focal point of the house, organizing circulation and spaces around it. At the bottom of the staircase is an open play area that leads to a designated toy and art room.

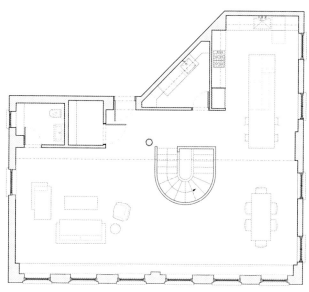

Upper-floor plan

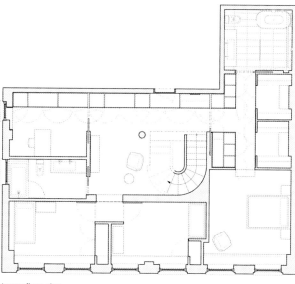

Lower-floor plan

013

White enhances the architectural character of a space and reflects light to create a bright atmosphere that can compensate for the limited amount of light.

014

Floating vanities and wall-mounted fixtures extend the open character of a loft space into a bathroom. This quality is further enhanced with the use of wall-to-wall mirrors.

The founders of Superpozycja Architekci faced the challenge of transforming a loft that was almost in ruins into a modern and functional apartment.

Aiming at maximizing space, they took advantage of the very high ceilings to build an upper floor with a bedroom, walk-in closet, and storage space. Several skylights on the roof bathe the space in light, enhancing the feeling of spaciousness and creating a warm and welcoming atmosphere.

Attic in Gliwice

Superpozycja Architekci

Gliwice, Poland

© Przemyslaw Skora

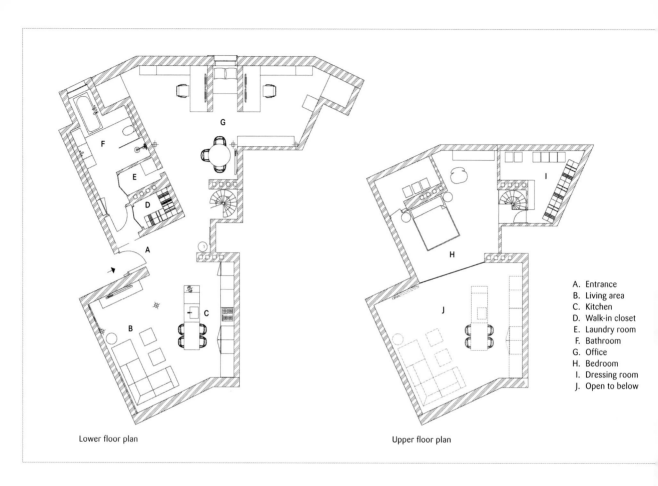

A. Entrance
B. Living area
C. Kitchen
D. Walk-in closet
E. Laundry room
F. Bathroom
G. Office
H. Bedroom
I. Dressing room
J. Open to below

Lower floor plan

Upper floor plan

015

A round table was chosen to take advantage of the corner. This type of table adjusts to any space—they are practical and make the room seem larger.

To retain the essence of the space, the old structures of the outer shell as well as the brick walls have been preserved. In addition, the wood from the demolition has been used to construct tables and countertops.

As if it were a classical canopy, the wooden structure is used to frame the bed in the bedroom and define the space. What's more, it breaks up the uniform neutral color, providing warmth and an interesting contrast of textures.

An old laundry room was transformed into a bathroom, utility room, and a spare walk-in closet. The architects decided to also expose bricks in the bathroom and to paint them in graphite.

The extensive remodel of a loft reveals a bold, sculptural, and open living space. Once a three-bedroom, dark renovation from the '80s, the loft was turned into a bright one-bedroom with one-and-a-half bathrooms, responding to the new occupant's requirements. The new design optimizes space and makes the most of natural light. A narrow and long entry hallway funnels out to a surprisingly generous open space with windows on two walls.

Chinatown Loft

Buro Koray Duman

New York, New York, United States

© Peter Murdoch

The interior space is divided by a sculptural wave-like wall that contains the laundry, storage space, and powder room. A vibrant, flat-green color contrasts with the highly textured finishes of the loft—mainly the brick walls and the wood floor—and enlivens the space.

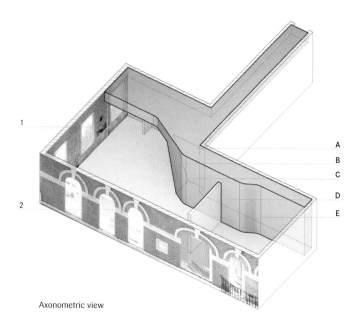

Axonometric view

A. Washer/Dryer
B. Pantry
C. Guest restroom
D. Bathroom
E. Closet

1. Existing brick wall
2. Existing building façade

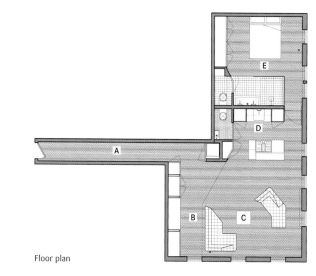

Floor plan

A. Entry
B. Office
C. Living area
D. Kitchen
E. Bedroom

017

Whitewashed brick walls soften up the raw industrial character of a space. Whitewashing is a solution to seal the surface of the brick wall and helps preserve the bricks.

Traces of vintage wallpaper in the
kitchen area were left to preserve bits
of history of the space, giving the newly
refurbished home a strong sense of
place and identity.

018

A splash of vibrant colors transforms any dull room into a dramatic space. However, vibrant colors draw the eye and can be overwhelming if used for more than just an accent. For this reason, avoid using them on work surfaces.

019

Brick walls add texture and character to a space, acting as focal points. They can also be painted to reduce their visual impact, allowing them to blend with the rest of a room's décor.

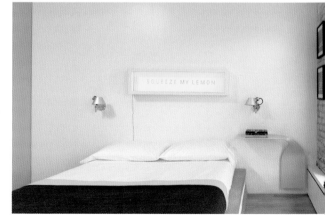

020

The tile in the powder room is a bas-relief honeycomb. Wall tiles set the atmosphere in a room. Available in ceramic, glass, and stone, they come in a wide range of shapes and finishes— matte or glossy—adding color and texture to suit any taste.

Contemporary Loft

ZPZ Partners
Modena, Italy
© Sarah Angel and ZPZ Partners

The essence of this project is the dialogue between the antique furniture—family heirlooms dating from the 17th, 18th, and 19th centuries—and a contemporary aesthetic and lifestyle.

This 2,690-square-foot loft, located in the historic center of Modena, occupies the top floor of an old building. A wide glass window opens onto a substantial terrace, flooding a large space with light, its continuity only breached by the two lit courtyards. The basic idea was to create a white monochrome scenario using a wide variety of materials: brick, matte varnished services, wood, glass, and metal.

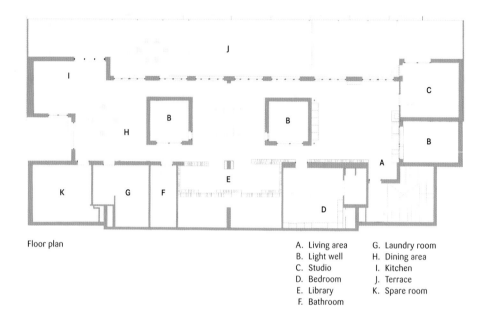

Floor plan

A. Living area
B. Light well
C. Studio
D. Bedroom
E. Library
F. Bathroom

G. Laundry room
H. Dining area
I. Kitchen
J. Terrace
K. Spare room

The two light wells break the long living area into three areas. The resulting areas have proportions that are better adapted to human scale and to the activities that take place in them.

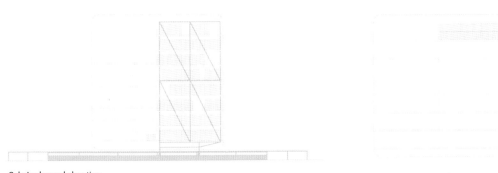

Cube's plan and elevation

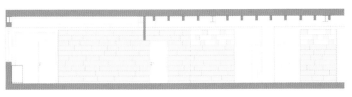

Section A-A

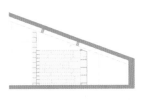

Section D-D

Section B-B

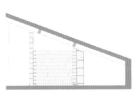

Section D-D with movable bookshelves

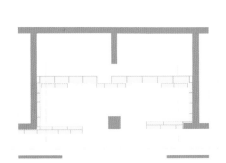

Library plan

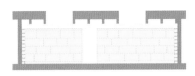

Section C-C

Section E-E

The white base is used to shelter antique furniture, without introducing new colors, creating what is an essentially bichromatic setting.

021

The alignment of openings connecting adjacent spaces and continuous elements that pass these openings reinforces the perspective, suggesting depth.

022

Monochromatic color schemes open the possibility of exploring other surface treatments such as texture. Our perception of texture is influenced by light, which reveals the qualities of the surface: rough, smooth, glossy, or matte.

The owner has a collection of 27,000 CDs and DVDs. A glossy, lacquered central cube with sliding shelves contains part of it. The remainder is distributed over 115 feet of shelving.

Light also brings together the monochromatic scene. The lamps have primary forms and are devoid of color— transparent or opaque spheres provide only light to the rooms, without adding other hues or materials.

023

A flexible variant of a terrace canopy is a simple textile piece, which can be unfurled to protect from the scorching heat of the summer. Out of season, the fabric can be pulled back or even removed and stored until the next good weather season.

Penthouse V

destilat ARCHITECTURE + DESIGN

Pörtschach, Austria

© destilat

In the course of the restoration of the Werzer cinema in Pörtschach, designed by the famous architect Franz Baumgartner in 1930, part of the truss was raised to form a spacious loft.

This 2,690-square-foot apartment is the holiday home of a German family of seven. One of the project's main challenges was to highlight the almost-twenty-foot-high living room ceiling while still creating a welcoming and comfortable atmosphere. Wooden floors, soft gray hues, and splendid white surfaces are the foundation for creating a serene and harmonious atmosphere.

Floor plan

0   3   6   9   12   15 ft

Surrounded by the children's rooms,
guest room, and master bedroom is a
spacious living area, including an open
kitchen, which has become the center
of the dwelling.

024

Light colors seem to expand the limits of a space, while dark colors tend to make things look heavy. These are clues that contribute to the creation of the desired appearance and atmosphere of a space.

The finish of the kitchen, using Eternit fiber cement panels, is a tribute to Austrian postwar architecture. The gently undulating lines of the drawers add a touch of freshness to the design.

025

Scale and proportion have a strong impact on the perception of a space and its functionality. A space can look tall and narrow, or low and wide. There is no wrong or right. It all comes down to what effect we want to create.

Loft LK

OLIVIER CHABAUD
ARCHITECTES

Paris, France

© Philippe Harden

Located on the fifth floor of a former car garage, Loft LK is an open space accommodating well-defined functions organized between outdoor spaces at opposite ends. Loft LK maintains the essence of the original space, exposing the raw concrete ceiling and using partitions only when absolutely necessary. The selection of materials—including glass, natural wood, white paint, and stainless steel—is in agreement with this aesthetic; the subtle lighting scheme complements the natural light that reaches the interior; together, they contribute to the creation of a unified space, both conceptually and physically.

From the entrance, the circulation is guided toward a large sunroom and a terrace beyond, passing by an open kitchen–living–dining area. The loft also enjoys a second outdoor space at the opposite end, accessible through the bedroom.

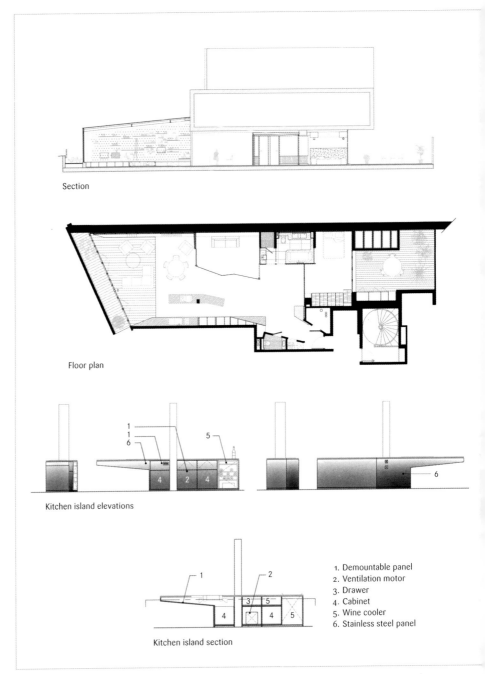

Section

Floor plan

Kitchen island elevations

Kitchen island section

1. Demountable panel
2. Ventilation motor
3. Drawer
4. Cabinet
5. Wine cooler
6. Stainless steel panel

The raw concrete contrasts with the white satin finish of the floor. Far from interfering with the unity of the space, this contrast enriches the loft with texture.

026

A subtle lighting design accentuates the distinction between existing and new elements, while enhancing the color and texture nuances of the materials.

027

New and preexisting elements are used to complement one another, as in the kitchen island, designed around an existing column.

028

With half walls—half solid and half glass—bathrooms and bedrooms can be closed or open to adjacent rooms by means of shutters or blinds. The lower half allows for furniture and plumbing fixtures to be installed.

While the loft is mostly open, the
design includes a series of fixed
and sliding panels, plus swing doors,
made predominantly of glass, in order
to articulate the different areas. If
desired, curtains can be added, to
enhance privacy.

029

No matter the size of a terrace, it will open up a loft space even more and provide ventilation. The transition between the two is a design aspect that needs to be looked at closely. Indoor and outdoor floors can be flush or at different levels.

This "inverse triplex" is designed for a family who loves to entertain. It embraces diverse materials, kinetic interventions, and a highly developed sense of the unexpected. The original space was transformed into a programmatic sequence to accommodate different functions and moods, from public at the front to private in the back. To adapt a low basement and sub-basement for living, the rear floors were demolished and reconstructed to allow for three full-height levels.

White Street Loft

Work Architecture Company

New York, New York,
United States

© Bruce Damonte

The design reinvents a typical steel- and glass industrial skylight at the rear of the loft, running the width of the building; it distributes light among all the levels, providing light-filled quarters for the children, and creating an outdoor courtyard at the master bedroom level below.

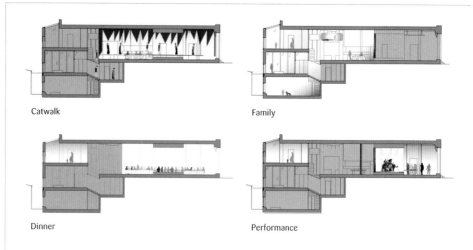

Catwalk

Family

Dinner

Performance

Diagrams showing possible scenarios for using the apartment

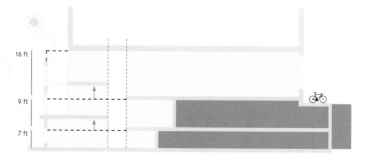

16 ft

9 ft

7 ft

Floor-realignment diagram

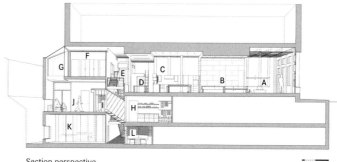

A. Living room
B. Bamboo-lined bar
C. Dining room
D. Games table
E. Dog elevator
F. Kid's bedroom
G. Open to master bedroom
H. Her closet
I. His closet
J. Master bedroom
K. Guest bedroom
L. Tequila nook

Section perspective

0   5   10 ft

First floor plan

A. Living room
B. Bamboo-lined bar
C. Powder room
D. Pantry
E. Dining room
F. Kitchen
G. Games table
H. Family/TV
I. Bathroom/Sleeping loft above
J. Dog elevator
K. Children's bedroom
L. Children's bathroom
M. Children's study area with light well
N. Open to patio
O. Shower
P. Open to master bedroom below

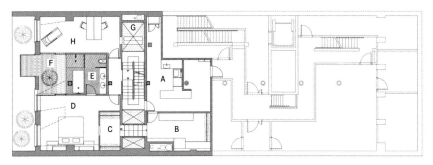

Cellar floor plan

A. Laundry
B. Her closet
C. His closet
D. Master bedroom
E. Master bathroom
F. Exterior deck
G. Dog elevator
H. Office/Gym

Subcellar floor plan

A. Guest bedroom
B. Tequila nook
C. Guest bathroom
D. Nanny's bathroom
E. Nanny's room
F. Children's playroom
G. Dog elevator
H. Stage

0   5   10 ft

The front-most section, at street level, is a loft-like living area that features white-resin floors and sixteen-foot ceilings; further in is a bamboo-lined box with built-in storage and motorized tables that rise from the floor for Japanese-style dining. These unique tables align, and can be joined together for large dinner parties, or to serve as a catwalk.

030

Areas can be delimited by color, setting the mood for a spatial experience different to that outside a designated area. This avoids the use of furniture such as consoles to divide areas, but may interfere in the comfortable flow of circulation.

031

Stainless steel's durability and resistance to heat and abrasion make it a perfect kitchen material. It's also versatile: at home in industrial or sleek settings.

Past the kitchen and dining area, before the stairwell, a ring with curved felt-covered walls, floor, and ceiling provides a comfortable media room and a kids-only sleeping loft.

A dramatic stairwell light shaft marks the level-shift, dividing front and back, while providing circulation between them. The circulation section also includes a translucent bridge connecting the master bedroom to a large closet and a doghouse/elevator for moving tired dogs, and snacks and toys between floor levels.

032

The combination of large windows and skylights creates spaces where light, coming from different sources, reaches every corner uniformly. Translucent partitions will go a step further, allowing light into a space that may require privacy.

033

Half windows placed just above a foundation wall and solar tubes are options to be considered to bring light into a dark basement. The best possible situation is, however, having access to a courtyard, which will open up the space.

Fractal Pad

Architecture in Formation

New York, New York,
United States

© Architecture in Formation

The client, a young and successful Wall Street broker, wanted
to convert his Tribeca apartment into an internal landscape.
The architects conceived this dwelling as a daily return to
Plato's cavern: a break from outside stress through the creation
of an abstract, all-enveloping, domestic landscape, where light
and shadow could be uniquely appreciated for their beauty and
mystery, and the outside world would cease to exist. The result
is a sumptuous oasis for lovers of geometry and mathematics
where harmony reigns.

034

A symmetrical arrangement
of furniture contributes to
a sense of balance and rest,
even if the furnishings are
not exactly the same.

The new, striking design uses the contrast between the original concrete columns and the red mahogany floor to evoke, at once, a futuristic private plane and a primordial cavern.

035

The lack of natural light wasn't a problem for the architects, who addressed it perfectly with indirect lighting. This design solution can also reinforce the geometry of a space.

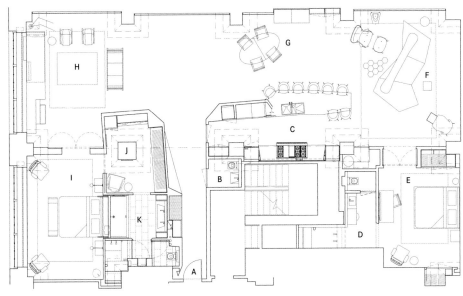

Floor plan

A. Entrance
B. Powder room
C. Kitchen
D. Bathroom
E. Bedroom
F. Media area
G. Dining area
H. Living area
I. Master bedroom
J. Dressing room
K. Master bathroom

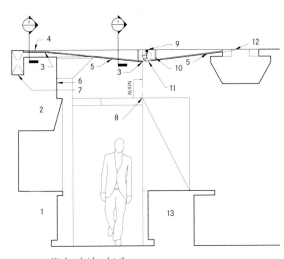

Kitchen bridge details

1. Range
2. Hood
3. Fold
4. Double layer of gypsum wallboard. Full depth of HVAC slot
5. Gypsum Wallboard
6. Line of cabinets
7. HVAC duct
8. Corner of floating ceiling
9. Plywood nailer
10. Light box interior painted. Gypsum wallboard painted flat white
11. Light slot
12. Edge of bridge to be trimmed for cloud base
13. Lower cabinets

Align
Centerline of fold point, corner of floating ceiling
Centerline of room

036

According to the American Lighting Association, there are three lighting types that are generally used in a home: ambient, task, and accent. Each has specific functions, ranging from a primary source of light to narrowed focused lighting.

037

Angular shapes are dynamic. Materials and lighting can reinforce this effect, creating false perspectives with stunning results.

Tribeca Loft

GRADE

New York, New York,
United States

© Francis Dzikowski,
Michael Weber

The design challenge for this project consisted of the addition
of a floor to a duplex that had been previously remodeled by
the same designers who were commissioned for the addition.
The addition, a 2,000-square-foot space directly below the
duplex, had to blend with the character of the duplex, a
dynamic environment ideal for hosting a variety of social
gatherings. It had to accommodate children's bedrooms,
along with a master suite and a dressing room.

038

You can expose original features of a space such as brick walls and roof trusses as a wink to its original design. However, think about how much of these features you want to expose so that they blend in well with the new design.

The use of unique materials throughout the loft expresses the ambitions of an avant-garde social setting; in juxtaposition the use of warm, soft materials establishes the innate qualities of a home.

039

As kitchens increasingly become the center of family social life, lighting design must support a variety of activities—thus, the mix here of general, task, and accent lighting.

To Do List
pick up kids from
Drop off Dry Clean
Doctor Appt
Take Dog to Vet
Gro
App
Mi
Bu
Pap

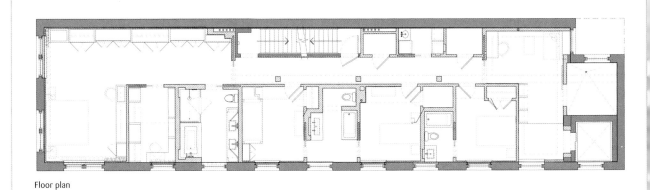

Floor plan

The scope of work involved the
repositioning of the existing columns
in order to create a single-loaded
hall. This allowed for the design of
reasonably proportioned bedrooms
and bathrooms and their placement
along a wall with windows.

The use of high-end materials, such as Italian black marble, along with meticulous attention to detail, lend the bathrooms a sexy, hotel-like appeal.

040

You can bring natural light deep into your house by making a staircase as open as possible. This can be achieved assuming there is a source of light at the top of the staircase.

This project consisted of an extensive loft remodel. The design team was given creative freedom to explore the possibilities that the existing space could offer, with the condition that the design include an indoor pool. Not only was this requirement met, but the existing space was transformed into a spacious, bright split-level home, taking advantage of the tall ceilings. Glass partitions, large windows, and a thoughtful lighting design combined to achieve optimal results with the available space.

Loft with Indoor Pool

AreaArquitectura.Design
Requena, Spain
© Juan David Fuertes Garcia

The living room has views of the split level: an open space accommodating the master bedroom, with access to the pool on the lower level, and a kitchen and dining area with access to a terrace on the upper level.

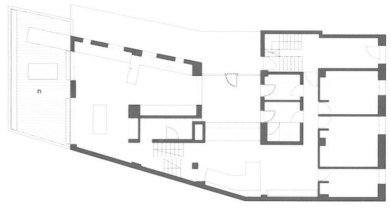

Upper-floor plan

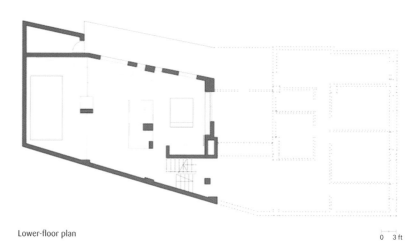

Lower-floor plan

0   3 ft

041

Floating staircases have a sculptural character that makes them a focus of attention. They allow visual connection between levels, and let light beam through, creating an airy feel.

Both the kitchen and the dining area, next to the terrace, benefit from abundant natural light. Lighting in these areas is balanced out by the light coming from the windows above the kitchen counter.

042

Available in sheer, translucent, block-out fabrics, and in many colors, roller blinds can suit any décor. It is worth noting that block-out fabrics offer a solution to climate control, protecting furniture from fading due to sunlight.

The minimal approach of the other rooms is carried through to the master bedroom, where the separation of functions is achieved with frosted-glass partitions and sliding panels. The continuous desk along the wall with windows reinforces the effect.

043

The fact that the bathroom is generally a separate room even in open-plan homes like lofts should not be an obstacle to extending the open character into this room.

Loft in South Moravia

ORA

Mikulov, Czech Republic

© Jan Žaulodek

This loft is part of an old building in a school built at the end of the 19th century, located in a small town in South Moravia, known for its unique landscapes and wine. Under the Communist government, the hall space was distorted by new roofing cement in order to build a loft over it. A wonderful carved wooden cover was concealed, and the space was divided into multiple floors. The aim, once the space had been refurbished, was to entirely restore it to its original state.

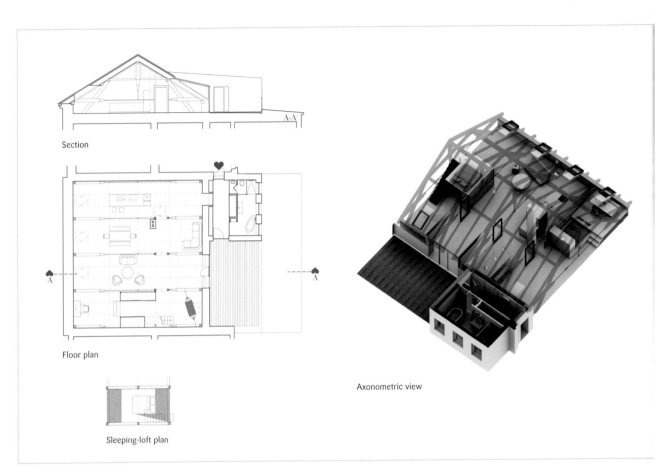

Section

Floor plan

Sleeping-loft plan

Axonometric view

044

The renovation of historic buildings is generally guided by building regulations aimed at maintaining the original character of a structure.

The wooden gabled roof, besides being the space's main decorative element, allowed for the construction of huge skylights, flooding it with light.

045

An attic can offer additional living area that will serve varied needs, not limited to the usual storage space. Make the most of the cozy and attractive space under a gable roof.

The space was segmented by tensioning steel rods. To find a way of crossing them, without altering their use, steel frames were introduced as if they were doors.

This project refurbished the original space—a luminous rectangular "aisle" with a gable roof resting on a structure of trusses and timber mullions—to provide it with new uses and new aesthetics while respecting its preexisting components. To achieve inner continuity, two partitions were demolished resulting in a large, clear, open space. A large canopy separates the sleeping area from the other rooms. This component contains wardrobes, a bed, a fireplace, and a staircase ascending to the "refuge," which is the canopy cover. So as not to disturb the space's essence, the walls were left untouched.

House HR

Olalquiaga Arquitectos

Madrid, Spain

© Miguel de Guzmán

The walls of the façade were strengthened internally to isolate the dwelling and so they could lead to the other facilities without altering the original structure. Air conditioning was installed by using underfloor cold/heat conduction.

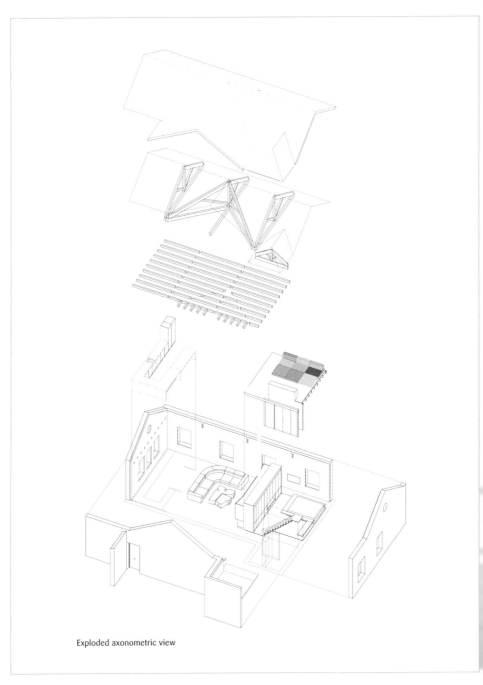

Exploded axonometric view

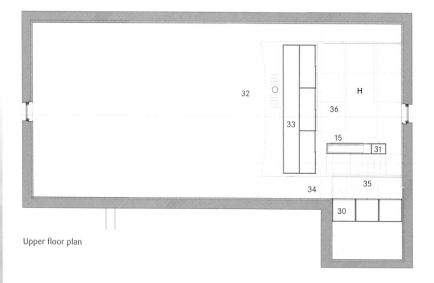

Upper floor plan

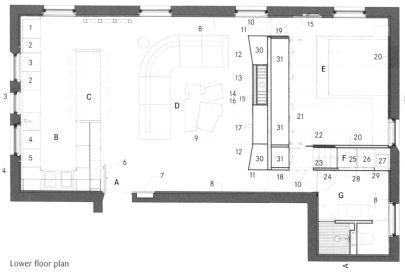

Lower floor plan

A. Entrance
B. Kitchen
C. Dining area
D. Living area

E. Bedroom
F. Laundry room
G. Bathroom
H. Spare room

1. Refrigerator
2. Freezer
3. Wine cabinet
4. Dishwasher
5. Oven
6. Wood entry door, painted white, semi-gloss finish on the interior side. Exterior side to match original. Laminated frosted-glass transom
7. MDF door to electric meter, painted white, semi-gloss finish
8. Baseboard, painted white, semi-gloss finish
9. Polished cement flooring
10. Stainless steel plate, flush with wall
11. MDF door, painted white, semi-gloss finish
12. MDF board, zinc-clad, exterior side painted anthracite color, and interior side painted white, semi-gloss finish
13. MDF sliding door, zinc-clad, with patina on exterior side and painted white on the interior
14. Insulation
15. TV screen
16. Ventilated chamber
17. MDF swing door, zinc-clad, with patina on exterior side and painted white on the interior
18. MDF board, painted white, semi-gloss finish
19. MDF swing door, painted white, semi-gloss finish. Concealed hinges, recessed stainless steel handle, and stainless steel plate
20. MDF board, painted white, with horizontal grooving
21. Closet front in MDF, clad in bleached maple
22. MDF sliding door, painted white, semi-gloss finish
23. Solid pinewood treads, clear finish
24. Waterproof MDF door, painted white, semi-gloss finish. Recessed stainless steel handle and stainless steel plate
25. Washer
26. Dryer
27. Water heater
28. Waterproof MDF door, painted white, semi-gloss finish
29. Waterproof MDF board, painted white, semi-gloss finish
30. Storage
31. Closet
32. Ventilation hole
33. Planter
34. Glass guardrail
35. Laminated glass with translucent PVB
36. Pinewood-plank flooring, clear-stained

Section A

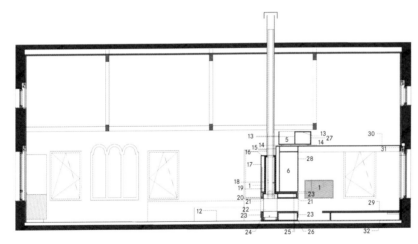

Section 3

Section 4

1. TV screen
2. Water heater
3. Dryer
4. Washer
5. Planter
6. Cabinet
7. Door frame painted white, semi gloss finish
8. Laminated glass with translucent PVB
9. Reinforced wood door, painted white, semi-gloss finish on the interior side, and fixed transom
10. Stainless steel handle
11. MDF door to electric meter, painted white, semi gloss finish
12. Polished cement flooring
13. MDF board, painted white, semi gloss finish
14. MDF planter base, painted white, semi gloss finish
15. MDF board, painted white, semi gloss finish
16. MDF board, painted white, semi gloss finish, with ventilation holes
17. MDF sliding door, zinc-clad with patina on exterior side, and painted white on the interior
18. Insulation
19. Ventilated chamber
20. MDF reveal, zinc clad, painted anthracite color
21. Steel box, painted to match reveal
22. Gas fireplace
23. Steel sheet, painted to match reveal
24. MDF baseboard, zinc clad, painted anthracite color
25. Fireplace surround formed by two layers of wallboard with rockwool insulation
26. MDF baseboard, clad in bleached maple
27. Sliding door, painted white, semi gloss finish
28. Closet front in MDF, clad in bleached maple
29. Bench and side table made of oak, stained dark
30. Pinewood-plank flooring, clear-stained
31. MDF board, painted white, with horizontal grooving
32. Oak-plank flooring, stained dark
33. Glass guardrail
34. Sliding side table made of oak, stained dark
35. Swing board in MDF, painted white, semi gloss finish, with rectangular holes
36. Sliding door in MDF, painted white, semi gloss finish
37. Solid pinewood beam
38. Framed picture
39. MDF door, painted white, semi gloss finish
40. Cabinet interior in MDF, with bleached-maple veneer
41. Glass shower door and stainless steel handle

046

A kitchen peninsula sets the boundaries for utilitarian culinary tasks. While separating the kitchen from the adjacent areas, a peninsula, like an island, can double as a surface for food preparation and for serving meals.

047

An area under a pitched roof cannot always be used as a habitable space—according to building regulations—due to headroom limitations. But this area can be turned into a cozy reading nook or an occasional sleeping loft, for instance.

048

Cove lighting can create a dramatic effect. It provides accent lighting to reveal color, texture, and form, or highlight certain elements. It can also be positioned to aim light in determined areas or on specific tasks.

This elegant 3,024-square-foot loft is located on the upper three floors of the west tower of one of the most emblematic buildings in London. The owner hired TG Studio to convert a standard apartment into a luxurious and elegant home.

The lower floor is occupied by the kitchen, dining room, a TV area, and two suites. The mezzanine features a comfortable living room and a collector's billiard table, which is the property of the homeowner. On the upper level can be found the main suite for relaxation and enjoying the excellent views.

St. Pancras Penthouse

TG-Studio

London, United Kingdom

© Peter Vile

The living and dining areas are elegantly furnished. Since large spaces can be prone to reverberation, the walls are lined with sound-deadening burlap.

The oak staircase not only connects the different floors of this loft but houses along its length an intimate reading corner and a spacious library and storage areas.

049

Location and views often
dictate the layout of a home.
Plan your rooms according to
these factors. In a multilevel
home, rooms on the highest
level usually afford the
best views.

Mezzanine-floor plan

Upper-floor plan

Lower-floor plan

050

As intimate as a bathroom may be, there is no reason why it could not reflect the open character of a loft. High ceilings are key and so is the use of glass instead of solid partitions to enhance the open feel.

On a platform above the living areas lies this welcoming open-plan bedroom, designed for the maximum enjoyment of the views of London.

Labahou

Planet Studio

Anduze, France

© Laurent Distel,
Ludovic Martial

This loft was a paper mill until the '90s. It fell into disuse, until Planet Studio transformed it into a contemporary home—with echoes of Provençal tradition.

The original factory consisted of two buildings on different levels. The first building, constructed with blocks of concrete over a traditional wooden frame, now serves as a living room with an open kitchen and several more levels where the everyday life of the dwelling takes place. The second, with metal beams, houses the bedrooms and a partially covered courtyard, whose roof was demolished to allow natural light to penetrate the bedrooms, bringing together all the dwelling's elements.

051

Consider installing a mezzanine, if you feel you could benefit from additional space in your home. Whether it is for storage, office space, or a bedroom, a mezzanine provides the ultimate solution to accommodate different functions.

The new owners wanted a modern home, but also one that would harmonize with its surroundings—hence the details of furnishings, beams, and wood, very typical of Provence.

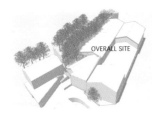

Site view

Scope of work

Organizational diagram

Structure
    1. Metal structure
    2. Wood structure

Views diagram

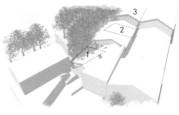

Exterior spaces
    1. Garden
    2. Patio
    3. Removed roof

Floor plan

A. Living area
B. Dining area
C. Kitchen (downstairs)/
    Office (upstairs)
D. Powder room
E. Bathroom
F. Vestibule
G. Bedroom

The fountain, which was a real find during the dwelling's construction, becomes an essential part of a garden with clear Mediterranean inspiration.

This loft was formerly a warehouse located over a bakery. The large open space, bathed in natural light, was the starting point for the project's inspiration, which sought an interplay of spaces while preserving specific characteristics rarely found in Paris. The original wood structure brings warmth to the atmosphere under the zinc roof. Inspired by "hipster" aesthetic, it is full of details, finishes, and furnishings selected in Spain, Sweden, and France, and designed by Multiarchi.

112 Belleville Hills

Multiarchi

Paris, France

© Christophe Gaubert

052

Small homes require a design approach to make the most of the space available. Often, best solutions are those that explore the multifunctionality of architectural elements—for example, a staircase that doubles as bookshelf.

053

In small spaces, avoid as much
as possible the construction of
solid partitions. This will make
the space feel cramped and
even smaller. Instead, choose
ephemeral solutions such as
sliding panels and curtains,
which offer more flexibility.

The hydraulic tiles in the bathroom evoke a classic Mediterranean residential style.

Loft in Bordeaux

Estudio Teresa Sapey

Bordeaux, France

© Estudio Teresa Sapey

Located in a former car garage in an industrial district, this loft is divided into two distinct areas by a swimming pool: one promotes social interaction, the other protects the intimacy of family life. The rooms are arranged around a central patio that establishes a vertical relationship among the various floor levels. The patio also enhances the height of the structure—which boasts original roof trusses—while allowing abundant natural light into the loft. The design incorporates efficient use of space, along with the clever application of color and graphics, inspiring well-being and cheer.

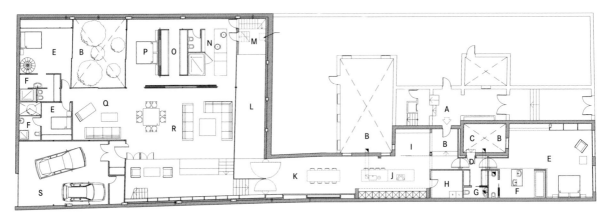

Floor plan

A. Entry
B. Entry hall
C. Courtyard
D. Vestibule
E. Bedroom
F. Bathroom
G. Powder room

H. Pantry
I. Cellar
J. Kitchen
K. Formal dining room
L. Pool
M. Mechanical room
N. Master bathroom

O. Walk-in closet
P. Master bedroom
Q. Lounge
R. Dining/Living area
S. Garage

054

The garage is often the neglected room of the house, and design attention rarely goes beyond the door. Loft in Bordeaux proves otherwise, with simple material and color touches.

055

Vinyl wall decals are a quick and fun way of personalizing your home. They stick easily to surfaces and require no preparation. Use them in any room of your home to create attractive accents.

056

Make the most of high ceilings with half floors. Not only will you add usable floor area to a space, but you will make a dynamic architectural statement.

The master bathroom features a sculptural Corian vanity that explores the extraordinary possibilities of this material with effortless elegance.

Loft Buzzi

Gianluca Centurani

Alessandria, Italy

© Gianluca Centurani

This three-apartment space on the top floor of a recently constructed building, together with an unused attic space, became a unique and impressive 4,305-square-foot loft, conceived with a modern rational and functional approach, with a terrace overlooking the heart of a small medieval town on the outskirts of Alessandria.

The loft is constructed around a central, double-height lounge, which the other rooms of the dwelling open onto. Furthermore it is also designed to provide complete interaction between the outside and the inside.

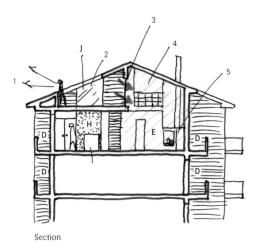

Section

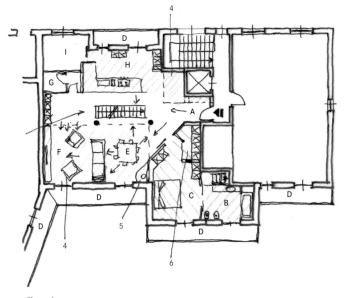

Floor plan

A. Entrance
B. Bathroom
C. Bedroom
D. Balcony
E. Dining area
F. Living area
G. Powder room
H. Kitchen
I. Laundry room
J. Terrace

1. Panoramic views
2. Window looking
   down to entrance
3. Window looking
   down to living
   and dining areas
4. Double height
5. Fireplace
6. Closet

057

Staircases do more than simply connect multiple levels: they can organize the space around them and can even be design features.

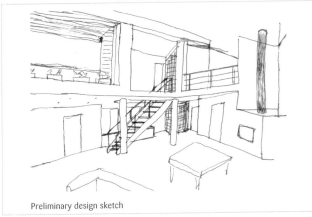

Preliminary design sketch

The shiny-red lacquered finish of the kitchen furniture, breaking with the neutral color palette used throughout the space, highlights volumes and marks out the spatial distribution.

058

The use of similar materials
throughout adjacent spaces
creates a sense of continuity:
they flow into one another
regardless of their function.

Cornlofts Triplex

B² Architecture

Prague, Czech Republic

© Michal Šeba

Located in Cornlofts, an old industrial building in Prague's Karlin district, this space, designed for both life and work, shuns conventional design with the goal of maximizing space and natural light.

Another starting point for redesigning this loft was to find a balance between old-fashioned industrial design and modern styles and materials. With that in mind, made-to-measure furnishings were designed combining vintage and modern in perfect harmony.

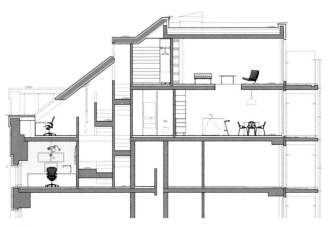

Building section

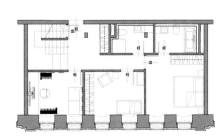

Ground floor plan

Second floor plan

Third floor plan

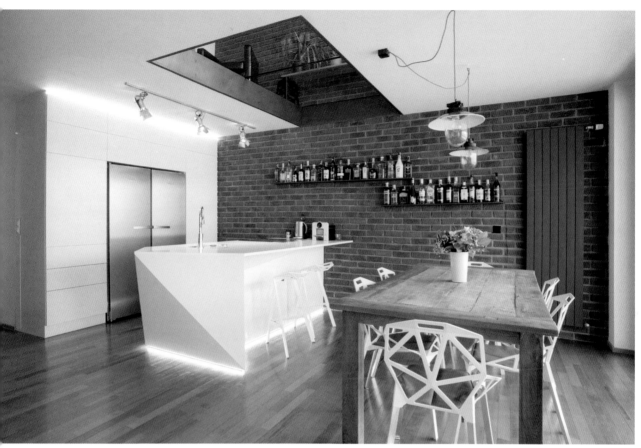

A brick wall, recycled wood table, and vintage-style hanging lamps contrast with the modern design of the island and kitchen module with LED lights to create the required stylistic balance.

Part of the original floor platform was replaced with glass in a central hollow. In this way, without wasting space, curious and unexpected vistas and more natural light are obtained.

059

Sound treatment of a music room can be as easy as the image above shows. Acoustic foam panels can be used on walls and ceilings to reduce noise transmission. Options offer a variety of shapes, sizes, thicknesses, and colors.

The translucent glass wardrobe doors have been carefully chosen. In addition to their originality and aesthetic beauty, since they allow light to pass, they provide a sense of breadth and visual continuity.

060

Screening off the toilet from the rest of the bathroom can be as simple as installing a thin partition in the finish of your choice—perhaps one already used in the room—if you don't (or can't) build a separate tiny room for it.

The design for this small living footage for a young fashion designer was aimed at optimizing the existing available space. The original layout consisted of a series of small rooms. The project involved the removal of various interior partitions and the insertion of a block splitting the space into two areas and accommodating multiple functions, including a staircase, an office, storage, and display. One side of the block is used as living area; the opposite makes room for a bedroom and a kitchen.

HIKE

SABO project
Paris, France
© SABO project

061

Attic spaces offer design opportunities that are as appealing as they are challenging. If headroom allows, consider putting in a middle floor that will increase the floor area and will be perfect as a sleeping loft.

Section

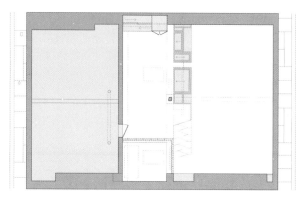

Upper floor plan

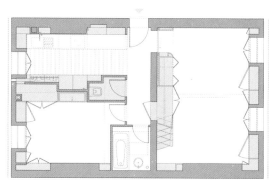

Lower floor plan

062

Alternating-tread staircase is a variation on a ladder stair. Since it is steeper than a regular staircase, it is a space-saver solution for small spaces.

In the kitchen, a stainless steel countertop is welded into place to extend over fifteen feet, providing plenty of work surface, all on one side. This striking linearity is pependicular to the striped, colorful flooring. Note the vertical garden that conveniently provides fresh herbs.

This loft is located in a building dating from 1913 and once occupied by a foundry. Following a residential refurbishment in 1980, all the cement columns and ceilings were covered up. Eliminating most of the partitions, as well as the false ceiling (which was more than three feet high), exposed the original building and enlarged the interior space. The new, more open space with its opacities and transparencies manages to bring natural light to all its corners without a loss of privacy. The new connections between rooms create a sense of continuity.

Doehler

SABO Project

Brooklyn, New York,
United States

© SABO Project

The large windows surrounding
the dwelling allow the landscape
to be enjoyed as if it were a picture,
and serve as a contrast to the
predominantly immaculate white
used throughout the dwelling.

063

A series of made-to-measure
wood containers extends from
the kitchen, bringing together
stairs, storage, lighting,
and work surfaces. This
multifunctional design allows
for the optimization of space.

The bathroom is designed using diamond-shaped tiles, which determine its size. Storage has been maximized with the use of white matte modules, whose smooth texture contrasts with the rough cement of the column.

Superfuture Design

ASZarchitetti

Florence, Italy
© ASZ architetti

This loft is part of an 18th-century convent that was subdivided to create living spaces. The subdivision left only one one room open to the outside, so there was just a single source of natural light. ASZ's renovation began by gutting the interior, eliminating all the accumulated space alterations of the centuries. By using a series of mezzanines pitched at different heights, the original 750-square-foot space was transformed into a space-efficient 1,070-square-foot loft.

064

In small spaces, it is best to limit the material and color selection to a minimum so as not to create an overwhelming atmosphere.

065

Multilevel structures are highly
effective at making the most
of available space. Particularly
suited to small spaces, so
common in dense urban
environments, this plan can
accommodate all the functions
of a living-working loft space.

Original 750-square-foot
lower level

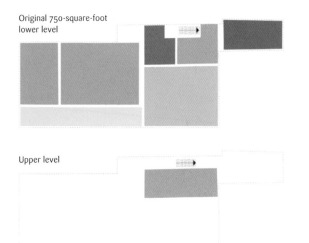

Project 1,070-square-foot
lower level

Upper level

Upper level

SCHEMES - Modification of the layout optimizing spaces

Living room		Entrance
Living/Dining room		Bathroom
Kitchen		Storage and connection
Master bedroom		

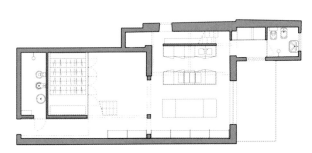

Lower-floor plan

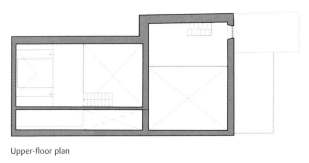

Upper-floor plan

066

Small spaces always come with challenges. How to organize different functions without overly fragmenting a space? Consider leaving the entire place open, only enclosing with minimal separations areas that require privacy.

This loft residence, belonging to a well-known photographer and his partner, is located in a former hat factory. A well-lit space was created, where the gray cement floor, together with the visible roof structure, reveals the building's industrial past. This is combined with ingeniously designed made-to-measure furniture, with matte surfaces, so only what is strictly necessary can be seen, thus creating a minimalist and orderly environment.

The kitchen, dining, and living areas form a unit separated from the private area by a double-leaf door.

Photographer's Loft

BRUZKUS BATEK

Berlin, Germany

© Bruzkus Batek Architekten

The kitchen furnishings in matte black with white detailing retain the minimalist aesthetic displayed by all the interior fittings. Only the veined-marble countertop brings a touch of contrast to the space.

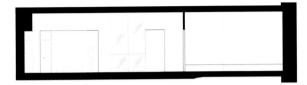

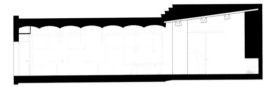

Longitudinal sections

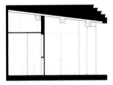

Cross section

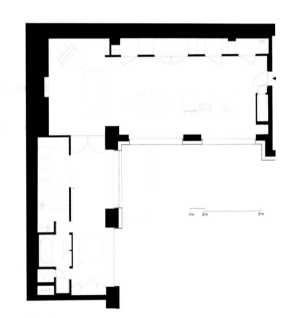

Floor plan

067

Wood paneling adds warmth to a space where "cold" materials, such as glass, stainless steel, and concrete, predominate. Also, its rich texture balances out the homogeneity of these predominant materials.

Loft in the Countryside

ASZ architetti

Florence, Italy

© ASZ architetti

ASZ's main goal in refurbishing this old barn in the mountains north of Florence was to balance its unique features with elegant contemporary aesthetics. The internal structure was completely redesigned to optimize its generous dimensions and acquire the maximum useful surface area while retaining its openness.

Care had to be taken to meet legal requirements for not only respecting the area's landscape but improving the building's resistance to seismic activity. A stainless steel roof was chosen to lighten the weight of the structure.

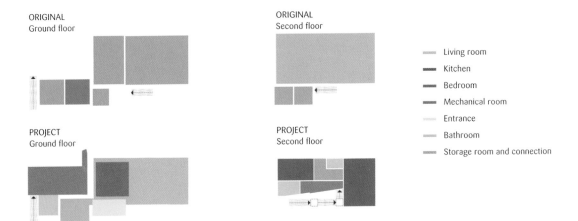

ORIGINAL
Ground floor

ORIGINAL
Second floor

PROJECT
Ground floor

PROJECT
Second floor

Living room
Kitchen
Bedroom
Mechanical room
Entrance
Bathroom
Storage room and connection

Diagram of space optimization

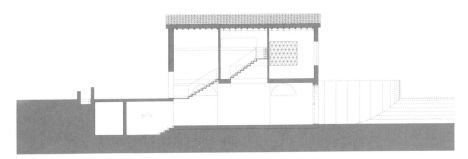

Longitudinal section

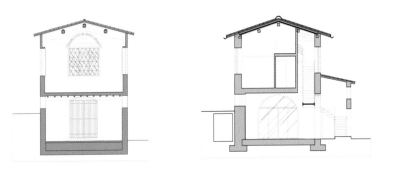

Cross sections

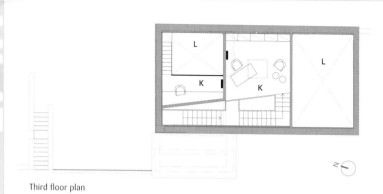

Third floor plan

068

The adaptation of a space to residential use is perhaps the most common type of change. This is mainly because of the high demand for quality housing and the desire to explore new and different lifestyles.

Second floor plan

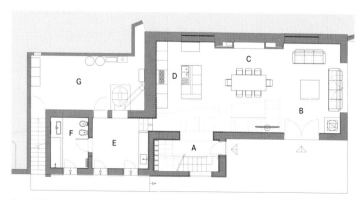

Ground floor plan

A. Entrance lobby
B. Living area
C. Dining area
D. Kitchen
E. Storage
F. Bathroom
G. Mechanical room
H. Vestibule
I. Bedroom
J. Walk-in closet
K. Studio
L. Open to below

069

In the event of a conversion, new support systems and elements of vertical circulation may be required to accommodate a new layout. Reinforcing existing walls may also be required if parts have been removed.

A concrete staircase enhances the spatial experience of the loft. It pierces the different planes that compose the interior, offering exciting and different views at every turn.

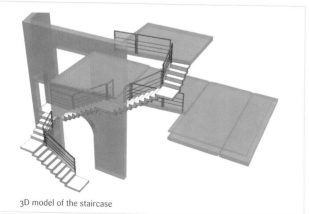

3D model of the staircase

Haruki's Apartment

The Goort

Mariupol, Ukraine

© The Goort

This single-room apartment of just over 376 square feet is located on the first floor of a two-story brick building in the historic city center.

Its current owners, a young couple, chose the format of a modern city apartment, spacious and bright, with minimal furniture but maximum functionality. The height of the ceiling, about thirteen feet, was key to solving the problem of space: it was converted into a lower (public) level and a second (private) one, connected by a functionally designed wood-and-iron staircase.

070

Maximize the storage capacity of your loft by taking advantage of the high ceilings. A rolling ladder that slides along the face of a tall cabinet will allow you to reach every corner.

There is not a separate work area as such—this function is served by a long shelf that runs along a wall, just beneath the windows. It doubles as a table for light meals in the kitchen area.

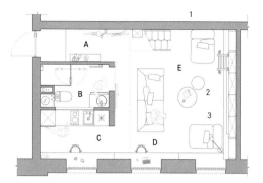

Lower floor plan

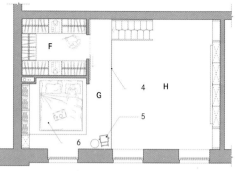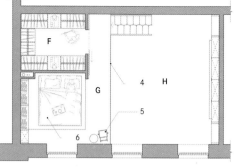

Upper floor plan

A. Entry hall	1. Goose-step ladder
B. Bathroom	2. Rolling ladder
C. Kitchen	3. Projection screen
D. Office	4. Glass railing
E. Lounge	5. Floor mirror
F. Walk-in closet	6. Podium bed
G. Bedroom	
H. Open to below	

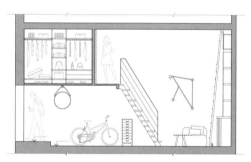

Section AA

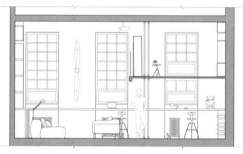

Section CC

Section BB

Section DD

Site plan

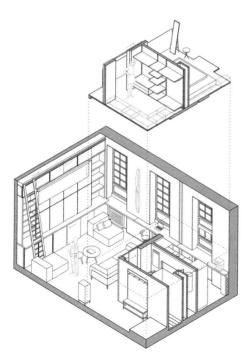

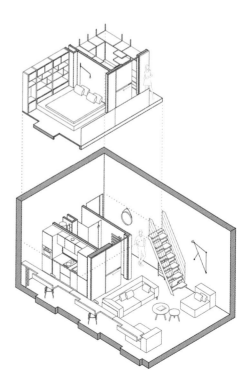

Isometric views

071

In architecture and interior design, function makes all the difference. When designing a space, it is critical to decide how the different functions will fit in an area, based on space adjacencies, traffic flow, and space sizes.

Kitchen appliances diagram

1. Compact washing machine
2. Electric single oven
3. Compact dishwasher
4. Electric cooktops
5. Built-in range hoods
6. Compact sink
7. Built-in refrigerator

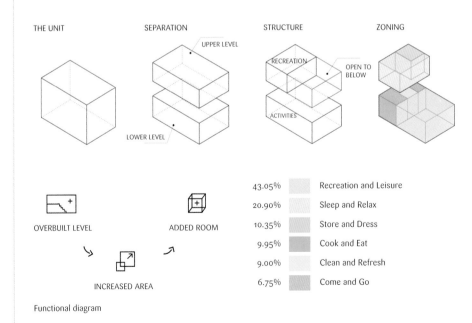

THE UNIT

SEPARATION

UPPER LEVEL

LOWER LEVEL

STRUCTURE

RECREATION

OPEN TO BELOW

ACTIVITIES

ZONING

OVERBUILT LEVEL

ADDED ROOM

INCREASED AREA

43.05% Recreation and Leisure
20.90% Sleep and Relax
10.35% Store and Dress
9.95%   Cook and Eat
9.00%   Clean and Refresh
6.75%   Come and Go

Functional diagram

072

Creative decorating ideas,
such as chalkboards or vinyl
wall decals, create unique
spaces that feel casual and
playful but also functional.

The phrase on the wall is a successful decorative supplement that gives personality to the space, since it conveys the feelings of the person living there. The typeface is very much in keeping with the style of the dwelling.

073

The blend of textures arising from the juxtaposition of new and recycled materials and objects creates an eclectic décor that is inviting and relaxed.

Industrial Loft

Diego Revollo

São Paulo, Brazil

© Alain Brugier

This loft combines the inherent industrial character of the existing space with comfort and contemporary design, contrasting materials and colors that exude warmth with others that boast rough industrial appeal. The walls and ceiling are conceived as a single envelope, enhancing the uniformity of the entire interior space. The individual parts that compose the loft's interior reflect an integrated whole in agreement with the desire to create self-organizational space.

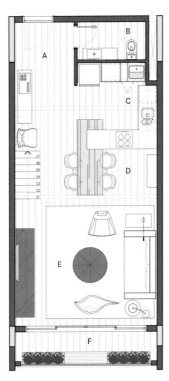

Lower floor plan

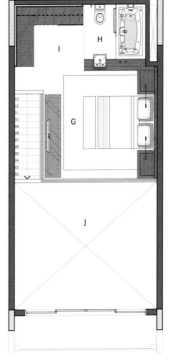

Upper floor plan

A. Entry hall
B. Powder room
C. Kitchen
D. Dining area
E. Living area
F. Terrace
G. Bedroom
H. Bathroom
I. Dressing area
J. Open to below

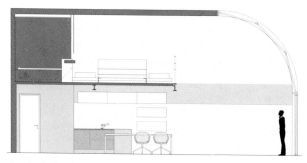

Longitudinal section 1

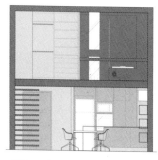

Cross section

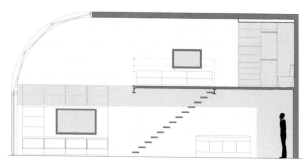

Longitudinal section 2

A glass wall that rounds off at the top to meet the ceiling makes the most of natural lighting. The room receives light from different angles evenly, creating a subtle play of light and shadow.

The layout is compact but doesn't look crowded, thanks to the efficient use of the available space and a selection of lightweight furniture

074

Windows may require some sort of protection from the sun, depending on their orientation. Protecting your windows will avoid heat gain and glare.

075

Designers often resort to
continuous elements as a
way to tie adjacent areas
together in order to ensure
the integrity of an open space.

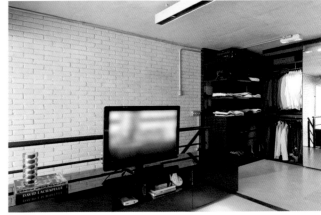

076

Sometimes all it takes is a glass pane between two areas that require separation but that you want to keep visually connected to emphasize continuity of space.

This loft, located in a historic 19th-century building, occupies one-third of the third floor, with large windows overlooking the city. The aim of the design was to preserve the original brick walls and emphasize the open, airy feeling created by the monumental windows and ceiling height.

The layout is simple: a one-bedroom dwelling, with open space for a living room, dining room/kitchen, guest bath, and laundry, and, above this, a study accessed via a staircase.

Downtown Loft

Michael Fitzhugh Architect

Traverse City, Michigan, United States

© Brian Confer

077

In order to create a mini-office, a breakfast bar has been designed for informal meals. A combination kitchen island/breakfast-bar overhang with stools is an increasingly popular space-saving solution.

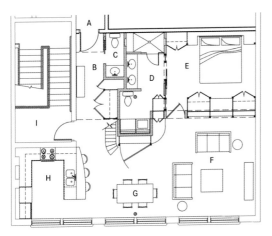

Main floor plan

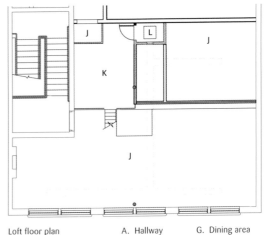

Loft floor plan

A. Hallway
B. Foyer
C. Powder room
D. Bathroom
E. Bedroom
F. Living area
G. Dining area
H. Kitchen
I. Exit stair
J. Open to below
K. Loft
L. HVAC room

078

An exposed brick wall, with its characteristic natural pigmentation, can serve as a focal point in any room. Far from communicating coldness, it adds texture and acts as a decorative element.

Staggered House

**schema architecture
& engineering**

Athens, Greece

© Marianna Athanasiadou

This house is located in Exarcheia, a suburb of Athens where many intellectuals and artists live. The essence of the project consisted in transforming the old dwelling, dark and restricted in size, into a single-family residence without compromising its personality.

To make the most of this confined space, to take advantage of its height, work was carried out vertically, leading to different levels within an open plan setup. Thanks to the careful selection of materials and furniture used, the old and the new combine seamlessly.

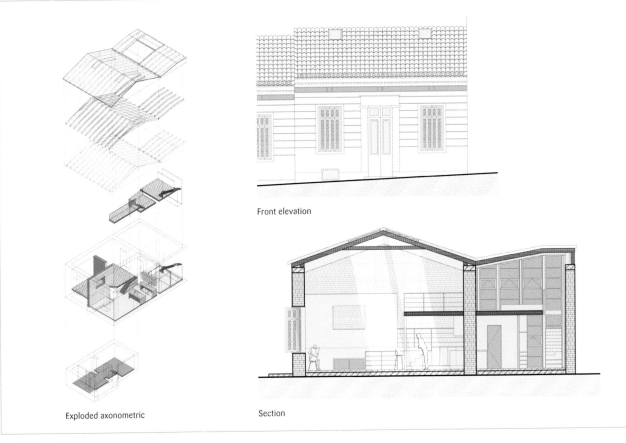

Front elevation

Exploded axonometric

Section

079

The challenge that comes with architectural conservation is to identify how change can occur without threatening the original character of a building.

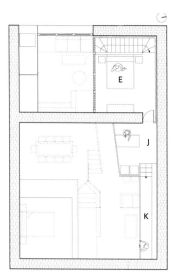

Second floor plan

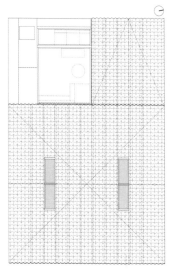

Roof plan

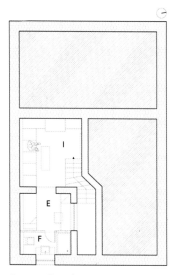

Basement floor plan

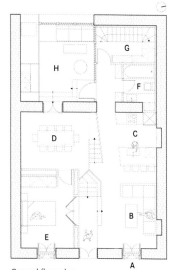

Ground floor plan

A. Entrance
B. Living room
C. Kitchen
D. Dining room
E. Bedroom
F. Bathroom
G. Dressing room
H. Terrace
I. Playroom
J. Office
K. Bookcase

The replacement of the metal doors with glass ones as well as adopting an open plan allows natural light to be enjoyed throughout the day.

080

The structural system of a historic building plays a major role in defining its character. It is further strengthened when its interior is fitted with new components that don't try to mimic the existing style, but rather contrast.

Designer Jaroslav Kašpar and architect Lucie Faturikova bought this apartment to refurbish and make into their home.

With a surface area of only 538 square feet, several walls were demolished to achieve a feeling of greater breadth. During the renovation, an old wood floor and brick walls were discovered; they were left visible to lend a vintage feel to the environment. The result: a rich and diverse atmosphere that triumphs over its small dimensions.

Little Big Flat

Lucie Faturíková (architect), Jaroslav Kašpar (interior designer)

Prague, Czech Republic

© Iveta Kopicová

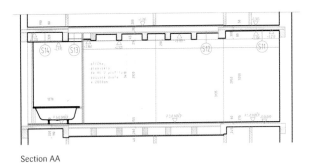

Section AA

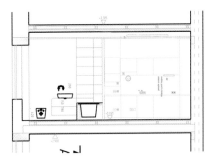

Section BB

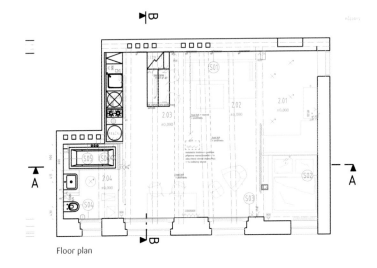

Floor plan

Instead of being covered, holes found in the brick walls were repurposed as niches for wine storage.

081

Amplify your home's storage
capacity by optimizing wall
space. Full-height built-in
cabinets are built-to-measure,
meaning that every inch is put
to good use.

The column and the wardrobe have been used to frame the sleeping area, which, even without walls, is still perfectly defined.

The only independent area is the bathroom. To optimize space, a translucent sliding door was installed, enhancing the sense of depth by diffusing light from the windows.

082

Cabinets with integrated lighting mounted between the mirror and the ceiling can come in handy if your bathroom's ceiling height allows it. They add storage space and provide task lighting above the vanity.

Loft in Athens

Studio NL

Athens, Greece

© Athanasia Leivaditou

A young journalist uses this loft space for work and leisure. Located on the top floor of a building in a residential area to the north of Athens, the apartment can act as a supplementary space to another, larger one located on the third floor, or as an independent space with a sofa bed, kitchen, and bathroom. Large sliding-glass doors lead out onto a bright terrace. To give a greater sense of breadth and depth, the same flooring material was installed both inside and outside on the terrace, with the effect of integrating the spaces.

A few beams, along with an LED lighting installation, were added to the existing wood decking. There are also electrical fittings for a computer, TV, stereo, and projector.

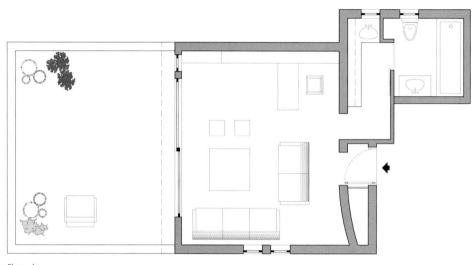

Floor plan

083

For maximum efficiency when space is limited, compact utilitarian rooms such as kitchens and bathrooms are the best choice, as they free up space for other areas that can lend to multiple functions and where one spends more time.

084

Vertical blinds are ideal for this space: they not only afford a view, but, with their rotating slats, they allow the lighting to be precisely modulated.

This loft apartment had the typical spatial configuration of a gothic house: elongated and narrow, with cramped corridors and spaces. It has been completely emptied out, and only the center staircase has been retained. It is now a bright, open space bounded by a longitudinal piece that runs throughout the level and performs multiple functions: furniture, kitchen, toilet, study, and wardrobe.

The end result: a white and diaphanous space acting as the container of a wooden box used for communications, and another, longer one, containing the necessary components for habitation.

Penthouse in A Coruña

sinaldaba

A Coruña, Spain

© Abraham Viqueira,
Juan Valiente

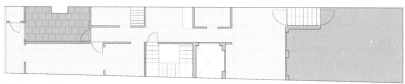

Existing conditions

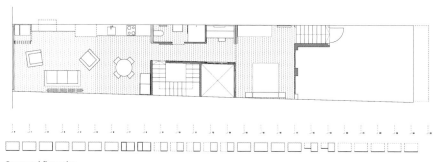

Proposed floor plan

085

Gutting the interior of an inefficient, overly compartmentalized layout is the first step toward the creation of a new space that favors natural light, efficient use of space, and circulation and amplitude.

The new layout provides spatial and visual continuity to the dwelling; all the rooms are connected. Uniform color and materials—silver fir wood is used throughout—further enhance the effect.

086

Horizontal cladding reinforces the elongated proportions of a space and the sense of perspective, adding visual depth, as opposed to vertical cladding, which emphasizes the height of a space.

To add the brightness so necessary for a space sharing these characteristics, the walls, floor, and ceiling, whose beams have been reinforced with metallic components, have all been painted white.

This project started out with a large, empty loft with sizable windows. The key innovation was to raise on a podium all spaces that required plumbing infrastructure, so that pipes could run unseen beneath the floor level.

The podium is framed by a bamboo strip extending from one side to another, defining the staircase and the surfaces, such as the kitchen countertop, in a sober and geometric fashion. In the main bedroom, the bamboo strip becomes the flooring, thus lending a sense of comfort and warmth.

Loft 02

EHTV architectes

Brussels, Belgium

© EHTV architectes + Herman Desmet

Section AA

Section BB

Section CC

Section DD

Section EE

Section FF

Section GG

Section II

Section HH

Section JJ

Floor plan

Pure and sober materials were chosen, resulting in a minimalist, seamless space. The floor is gray polyurethans, the walls are painted white, and the ceiling is unfinished cement.

087

Raised floors, sliding panels, and structures short of the ceiling allow for the creation of flexible spaces that can be used as needed, while preserving the open character of the original structure.

088

The functions of a bathroom are perhaps the only ones that require a separate room. In an open-plan home, like a loft, this can be used as an opportunity for the creation of a structure that organizes the overall layout.

This loft occupies part of the ground floor of an old palace in the heart of Padua. The project was inspired by the classic Italian city center, where a stroll through narrow streets continually reveals new and unexpected pleasures. The priority was to maximize interior light and retain the building's peculiarities, which meant undoing the arbitrary and often incoherent additions of generations of refurbishments.

Loft in Padua

MIDE architetti

Padua, Italy

© MIDE architetti

A sequence of continuous spaces has been created, with the shared spaces closer to the entrance and the intimate spaces farther back.

089

Given the predominance of white, the black used in the kitchen separates this area from the rest of the dwelling. This is an example of how a simple color contrast can act as a space divider, without the need for furniture or any other resource.

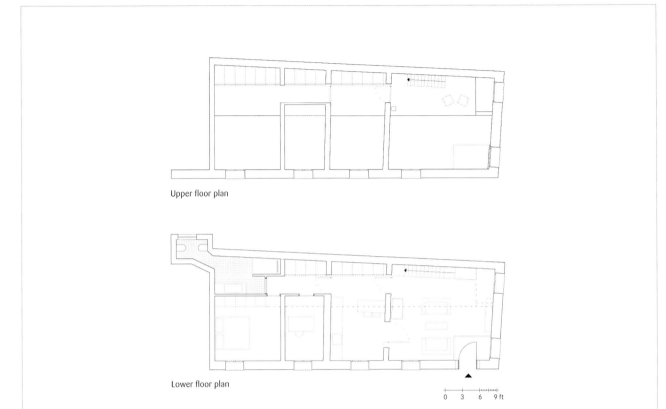

Upper floor plan

Lower floor plan

0   3   6   9 ft

090

Concentrating the staircase, storage space, and the bathroom along one long wall, as shown in the plans above, frees up valuable space, creating an environment that lends itself to different activities.

The refurbishment of the original wooden ceiling and the rediscovery of part of the brick wall are the common threads joining the rooms, contributing to a continuing contrast between the historic and the contemporary.

This loft is part of a project that aims to transform a series of industrial buildings into art galleries. It consists of a study gallery on the ground floor, and three live/work spaces for artists on the upper floor. The main challenge here was to retain the personality of the original buildings without surrendering innovation.

Bergamot Station

Brooks + Scarpa

Santa Monica, California, United States

© Marvin Rand, Benny Chan

Polished cement floors, walls painted
in a simple way, exposed steel trusses,
and metal cladding contribute to
a serene atmosphere, in which the
highlighted components build complex
textures and spaces.

A broad plane of corrugated metal is broken up by rectangular volumes of Lexan resin, cement blocks, and glass, creating an elegant composition.

South elevation

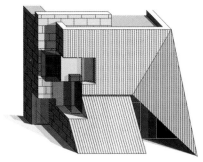

Axonometric view

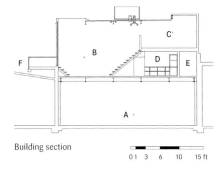

Building section

A. Gallery
B. Loft live/work space
C. Loft living area
D. Kitchen
E. Hall
F. Deck

0 1 3   6   10   15 ft

The ground floor is designed as a multipurpose open space. A separate entrance leads to the three upper units, where space and light have been maximized without sacrificing privacy.

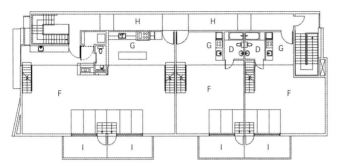

Loft floor plan

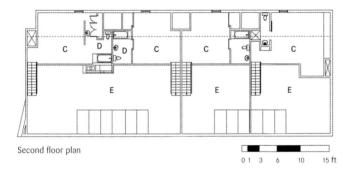

Second floor plan

0 1 3   6   10   15 ft

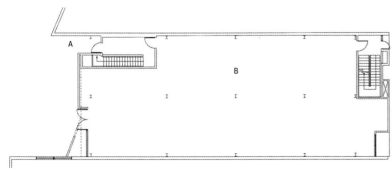

Ground floor plan

A. Entrance
B. Gallery
C. Loft living area
D. Bathroom
E. Open to below

F. Loft live/work
    space
G. Kitchen
H. Hall
I. Deck

091

Corrugated metal finds its way into residential construction, providing a space with an industrial aesthetic. Although it is not a common interior finish, it can make for an interesting ceiling, complementing concrete and glass surfaces.

Part of the corrugated metal roof has been replaced by glass so that light can penetrate every corner of the room.

Loft SanP

Paolo Larese architetto
Padova, Italy
© Matteo Sandi

This former printing press warehouse was converted into a loft that embraces the principles of postindustrial architecture. The scope of work involved stripping back some of the existing elements, in order to create new spaces adapted to new activities. The conversion included major changes that affected the structure, roofing, utility systems, and the organization of the space, all based on programmatic requirements. The result was a two-floor living space that boasts a coherent organization of functions, yet imparts a rich spatial complexity.

A two-level ground-floor plan accommodates a large open room on the ground floor, where a living, dining, and kitchen area overlooks an outdoor space. A raised floor gives room to an expansive sitting area with a fireplace. Its generous proportions—it features a double-height ceiling—stand in contrast to the more conventional living area.

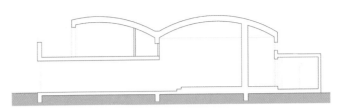

Section

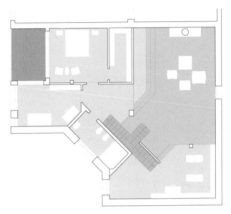

Upper floor plan

Lower floor plan

Architectural detailing and choice of materials go hand in hand, giving each individual element or surface a strong identity.

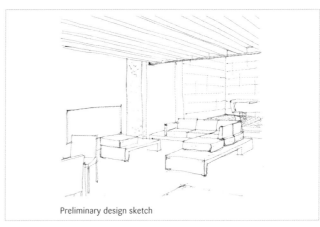

Preliminary design sketch

092

Continuous wall surfaces, low furniture, and ceiling beams create a perspective effect and accentuate the horizontality of a space.

093

Two different light sources can fill a room with uniform light. This minimizes contrast between light and shade and also reduces glare.

This multifunctional 861-square-foot space, currently serving as a guesthouse (it's connected to a 1,937-square-foot loft on the upper floor), is located in a historical 17th-century canal house in central Amsterdam.

An open space with high ceilings, it's all about contrast: modern structural designs are set against recovered brick walls and heavy wooden ceiling beams. From the back you can access a garden.

Loft Amsterdam Canal

Jeroen de Nijs BNI
Amsterdam, The Netherlands
© vanbelkomproducties

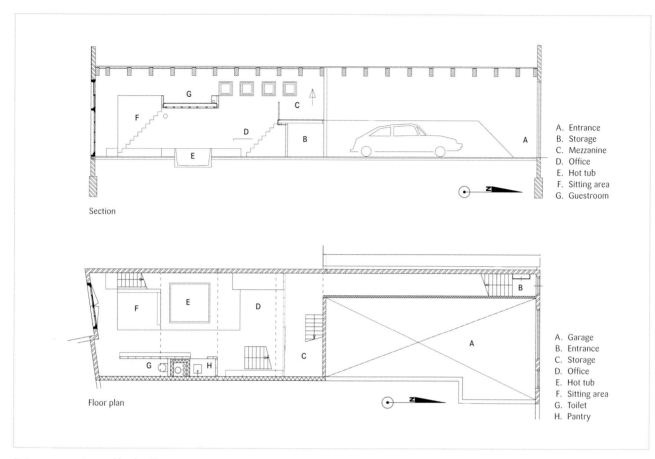

Section

A. Entrance
B. Storage
C. Mezzanine
D. Office
E. Hot tub
F. Sitting area
G. Guestroom

Floor plan

A. Garage
B. Entrance
C. Storage
D. Office
E. Hot tub
F. Sitting area
G. Toilet
H. Pantry

Staircases connect several levels with
different uses: work area, projection
corner, Jacuzzi, pantry, bedroom, and
toilet. This is a fun place waiting to
be explored.

094

Inserting architectural elements into an open-plan space can create a strong visual impact. Not only do these elements acquire a prominent role in the layout of the space, but also the space, as a container, stands out by contrast.

Computer-generated interior perspective views

095

Staircases can have multiple functions. Here, creative use was made of the space below by installing storage shelves.

Loft in Milan

Marco Dellatorre

Milan, Italy

© Marco Dellatorre

Marco Dellatorre designed this sixteen-foot-high loft in what was an old Milanese metal factory. His aim was to pay tribute to its original industrial use, preserving its open plan, but without falling into minimalism.

This dwelling defines perfectly the concept of an Italian-style loft: it is open and fluid, but at the same time intimate, warm, and seductive. There is no physical separation between the rooms, but the different areas, even functions, are defined by colors and materials.

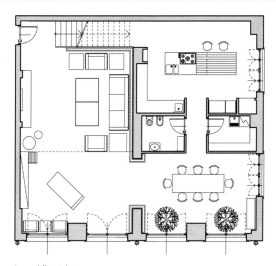

Ground floor plan

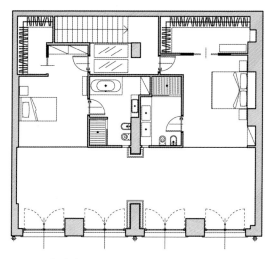

Mezzanine-level plan

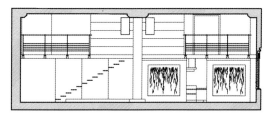

Longitudinal section

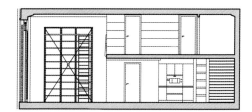

Cross section

096

Mezzanines offer the additional space of an extension. They also provide a loft with a great sense of volume created by the counterpoint with the double height ceiling.

The lounge is a real showcase of diverse materials, with dark-leather furniture and an oxidized-copper wall delivering the requisite ambient warmth.

The wall coloring, inspired by the typical *case cantonieri* of Italian railway tracks, and the treatment applied to it rekindle the essence of the past in a contemporary environment.

097

Finishes such as stainless steel, glass, and concrete are often associated with lofts because they generally remind us of the spatial atmosphere of industrial buildings.

The French oak flooring used in the bedroom was recycled from the old beams. Only the top layer was used, in order to preserve the marks showing the passage of time.

098

Adding style and visual interest in your bathroom is as easy as creating a focal point, using ceramic tiles to cover a floor or wall area. Don't overdo it. The result should be a balance between this focal point and the rest of the bathroom's décor.

An old car repair shop, being used for storage, was transformed into a living space by a designer for his own use. Drawing inspiration from the many magazine clippings he had collected over the years, and putting to good use his penchant for mixing old and new, he created a space based on his taste and his needs—chief among them the need to showcase his many collections in an informal way that didn't recall a museum.

Garage Loft

Bricks Studio
Amsterdam, The Netherlands
© Valentine Harmsen

099

Track lighting is a perfect solution for ceilings that do not allow for recessed fixtures. It is also useful in spaces that require movable and aimable lights, given its capability to provide both overall and task lighting.

The living area displays most of the designer's object collections, from furniture, framed art, books, and light fixtures to an early-20th-century railway station clock hanging from the ceiling.

Floor plan

Access to the loft is through the garage,
directly into the kitchen and dining area.
The one-story space is long and narrow.
With no windows along its side walls,
the space receives natural light primarily
from a small interior courtyard and
a large skylight above the living area.

100

Glass and steel window walls remind one of 19th-century greenhouses. Their charm along with their slender sightlines makes them attractive both as interior partitions and as boundaries between interior and exterior.

101

You can give vintage and recycled pieces new life in your home to create an environment with character and history; from a rustic look or a shabby chic vintage home to an interior with a contemporary appeal or industrial edge.

The bathroom, like any other space, contains a collection of antiques that are not just for show: the claw-foot tub and the workshop bench repurposed as vanity.

A former army barracks dating back to the reign of Kaiser Wilhelm II was transformed into a large residential complex that includes this loft, now home to a family with two children. This 4,305-square-foot area has been converted into a wide open space with differentiated living spaces and striking visual perspectives. Upon entering, a spacious area opens along the vertical and horizontal axes. An L-shaped gray translucent curtain separates the entrance from the living area, so the environments can be fused when required. Natural, warm materials and colors contrast with notes of pink, cubic volumes, and glass surfaces.

Loft ESN

Ippolito Fleitz Group

Esslingen, Germany

© Zooey Braun

102

Mirrored walls can transform
a room into a space where
reflection creates intriguing
visual effects and blur barriers.

The pattern of branches engraved in the mirrored walls echo the wooded surroundings, bringing this natural element into the interior of the home.

The ground floor is constructed around the dining area, clearly defined by a carpet, on which rests a long table, and a set of stylized hanging lamps.

103

If you are thinking of designing your kitchen, consider the visual composition. Besides practicality and function, the arrangement—in addition to form, color, and material—is what draws attention.

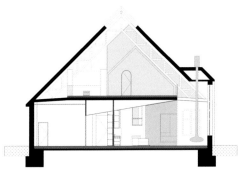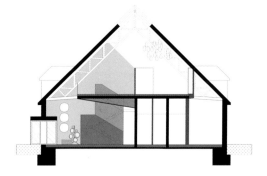

Sections

Lower floor plan

Upper floor plan

On the upper floor, the domain of the parents, is a work area that, far from being in a closed-off corner, is open-plan.

104

Use color wisely to bring out the spatial characteristics of a space and to create interesting visual effects. Light colors jump forward, while dark colors recede. This effect is visible when the two colors, light and dark, are juxtaposed.

The circular wall mirror expands the space, and reflects the interplay of lights created by the fragile spheres hanging from the ceiling.

Loft Biella

Federico Delrosso Architects

Biella, Italy

© Matteo Piazza

Loft Biella is one of the wings of an old textile workshop where a block was refurbished to accommodate Studio Delrosso. The most characteristic feature of this apartment, inhabited by the architect, is its movable dividers. On the ground floor, the space is divided partially along one side by wooden panels allowing certain sections to be closed off. This idea is repeated above, on the upper floor, where along the railing there are a series of centrally hinged panels permitting any space to flow or be sealed off according to need.

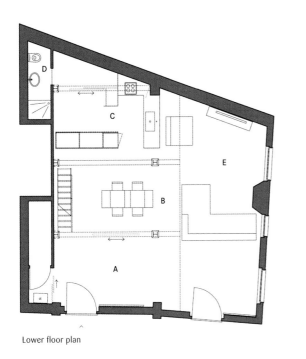

Lower floor plan

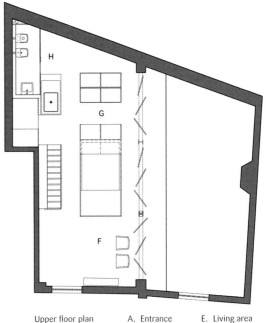

Upper floor plan

A. Entrance
B. Dining area
C. Kitchen
D. Bathroom

E. Living area
F. Bedroom
G. Dressing area
H. Bathroom

105

Freestanding modules create spaces within an existing shell. The classical approach, wherein kitchen furniture is secured to walls, is no longer the only available option.

The minimalistic staircase boasts an origami appearance, rising lightly. Its folded structures echo the corrugated-metal deck of the mezzanine.

106

In the manner of an old-
fashioned canopy, a lightweight
metal structure, sporting
a gauzy curtain, surrounds
the bed, creating a private
intimate space when desired.

Loft in Saint Petersburg

**Boris Lvovsky, Anna
Lvovskaya, Fedor Goreglyad/
DA Architects**

Saint Petersburg, Russia

© Polovkova Anna

This project's main idea was to create an integrated space rather than small, poorly lit, isolated units. To carry out this conversion, several subspaces were decorated with fissile mosaics, veneered birch, cement, and metal covering 3,013 square feet and forming part of a whole. The unique feature of this design is that the walls of the subspaces do not reach the ceiling, which emphasizes their isolation from one another without compromising their integral role in the larger space.

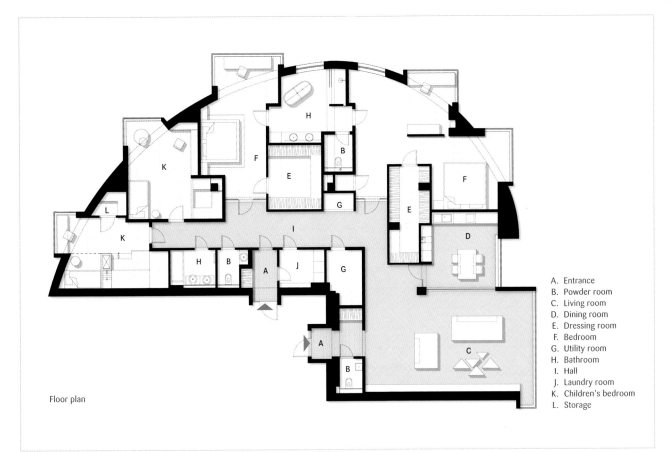

Floor plan

A. Entrance
B. Powder room
C. Living room
D. Dining room
E. Dressing room
F. Bedroom
G. Utility room
H. Bathroom
I. Hall
J. Laundry room
K. Children's bedroom
L. Storage

107

The compartmentalization of a space for the separation of activities can create a feeling of confinement. To minimize this problem, partitions can be designed to be short of the ceiling to highlight the effect of continuity of a space.

108

Use a palette of few tones to set the general mood of a room. Touches of color can be added to attract attention and enhance the aesthetics of a space.

Some of the subspaces are connected with smart glass—the glass changes from clear to translucent—allowing for the separation of private areas when required.

109

Texture, like color, can be used to create visual interest. It can enrich the color scheme that predominates in a space so that the unity of this space is maintained, or it can combine with an accent color for greater effect.

110

Wood breaks up the coldness of the cement and lends warmth to the environment, as well as creating an interesting color contrast.

Vegas Loft

Vladimir Radutny Architects

Las Vegas, Nevada,
United States

© Vladimir Radutny Architects

The owner of this loft bought it with the intention of exhibiting his large collection of paintings. The idea was to modify the perimeter, turning it into a continuous plane for his works. A number of areas were created in each of the window openings by adding small spaces within the new wall. To recover some of the lost surface, the areas for domestic use have been located strategically. Additionally, a wooden platform was built to run along the entire northwest perimeter, defining a new area within the open-plan space.

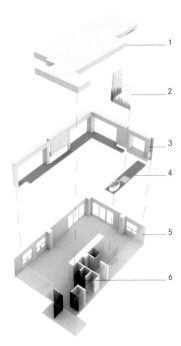

1

2

3

4

5

6

1. Altered dropped ceiling
2. New bedroom screen
3. New programmed perimeter
4. New raised platforms
5. Existing perimeter
6. Service area reconfigured

Axonometric view

Existing elevation

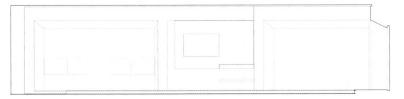

Proposed elevation

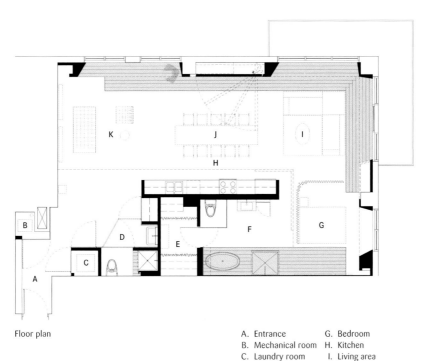

Floor plan

A. Entrance
B. Mechanical room
C. Laundry room
D. Guest bathroom
E. Walk-in closet
F. Bathroom
G. Bedroom
H. Kitchen
I. Living area
J. Dining area
K. Sitting area

111

The original plan of the loft was all fragmented. The removal of these partitions achieved an open space that connects the different areas within the loft, but also opened up the interior to the views.

A continuous raised platform along the perimeter of the loft defines a new area within the open plan. This new surface can be used for the display of artwork.

112

Consider painting a space in
the tones found in the artwork
that you are going to display
for a harmonious look. White
is, nonetheless, the safest
option that offers a neutral
backdrop for your artwork and
gives it the attention it deserves.

The entrance area was reconfigured,
and black metal panels were installed;
they can be moved to form either
a common area for hand-washing
or a second bathroom.

113

The thickening of an existing wall to accommodate functions of the home is a good space-saving solution. By doing so, you minimize the presence of freestanding elements that can cramp the space.

To give a greater feeling of
spaciousness, the false ceiling
was partially removed, exposing the
ventilation ducting and introducing
a modern, industrial aesthetic.

A wall was originally separating the bedroom from the bathroom. With its removal, not only is the bathroom connected to the bedroom, but it also receives abundant natural light.

An Oasis in the City

Dreimeta

Augsburg, Germany

© Steve Herud

Here is a real treasure in the heart of the urban jungle: a bungalow built in 1969 in a contemporary style surrounded by beautiful trees in the center of Augsburg. The goal was to include contemporary design elements, modern technology, and collectibles from around the world without compromising the house's original style.

The dwelling originally had two floors. When it was refurbished, a 592-square-foot third floor, made of wood, was added as a guest house.

114

Staircases can be an architectural feature that stands out for its sculptural qualities. It can be enhanced by a careful selection of artwork that brings out its style, colors, and materials to achieve a homogeneous atmosphere.

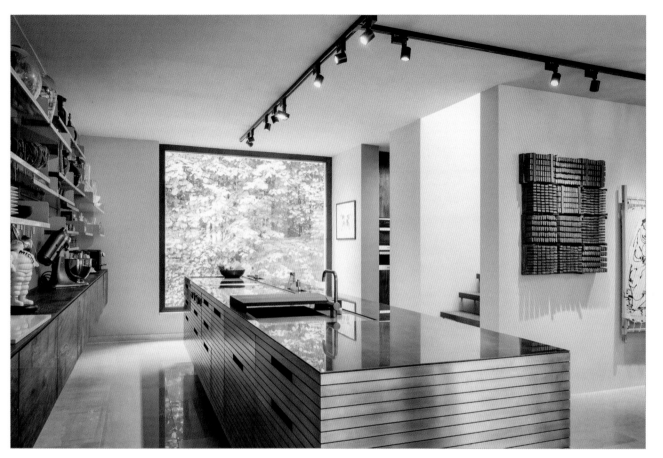

The kitchen, designed by its owner, features a picture window that frames a verdant scene, adding a crucial note of color to a predominantly neutral scheme.

115

Hanging fireplaces can add
visual interest to a space.
Because of their sleek design—
often spherical or ellipsoid—
they generally complement
contemporary interiors, but
they can also harmonize with
classic or rustic styles.

116

Reclaimed wood offers interesting opportunities for the design and creation of furniture. Its weathered surface gives the furniture that is made of this material a charming appeal that embraces distinctiveness and history.

A skylight has been opened in the roof of the guest bedroom, located just under the roof, which in addition to providing brightness helps save energy.

117

Floor-to-ceiling windows
minimize the boundaries
between spaces, enhancing
a sense of amplitude and
continuity between adjacent
interior spaces, as well as
highlighting the connection
between interior and exterior.

Amsterdam South Loft

Jeroen de Nijs BNI
Amsterdam, The Netherlands
© Jeroen de Nijs

This 2,152-square-foot loft, with an impressive balcony, is located on the top floor of an old office building converted into a residential unit.

In the center of the structure of columns forming it we find an impressive walnut wood module, which houses the lift leading to the dwelling, the staircase leading to the terrace, and the boiler room. The dwelling consists of two main areas: two bedrooms (each with its own bathroom) and an open living room connected to a kitchen. The luxurious selection of woods contrasts with the rawness of a space dominated by materials such as visible cement and brick.

118

Open-plan living areas boast spaciousness, but they have their own special challenges when it comes to furnishing them. Grouping furniture according to activities will help create cozy areas, so hard to obtain in loft spaces.

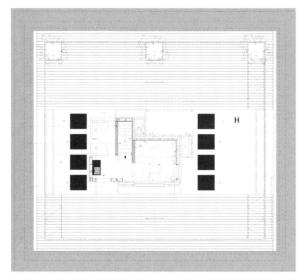

Roof-terrace plan

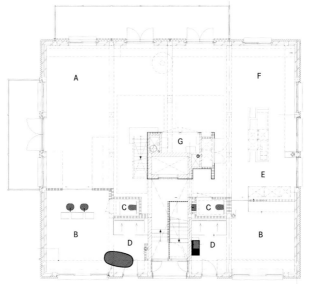

Floor plan

A. Living area
B. Bedroom
C. Toilet
D. Bathroom
E. Kitchen
F. Dining area
G. Mechanical room
H. Roof terrace

The low ceiling height necessitates that the heating system be located beneath the cement floor. Augmenting the system is a suspended fireplace that can distribute heat evenly throughout the entire room.

Computer-generated interior perspective

119

Built-ins are great space savers. As shown in the image, a deep bench can serve as a daybed, turning a small space into a convenient guestroom. The bench is also a container, adding to the storage capacity of the home.

120

Having a private and easily accessible bathroom adjacent to a bedroom is a clear commodity. En suite bathrooms have also become a much sought-after home asset that may increase the sale value of a property.

The light-filled loft apartment is complete with a generous roof terrace. Access to the terrace is through a small room, an ideal reading nook. The reduced dimensions of the room are compensated by the amplitude of the terrace that surrounds it.

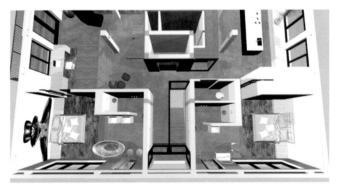

Computer-generated perspective views

The terrace has a living area, bar, barbecue, and shower. Abundant vegetation and a platform floor featuring artificial grass make it an oasis in the midst of the hustle and bustle of the city.

The aim, in this refurbishment of a former textile factory, was to retain its diaphanous nature while also providing some measure of intimacy. Thus on the ground floor we find a completely open area where environments, delimited only by different materials used, flow into one another; plus a night area, consisting of two rooms and a bathroom. The upper floor, in direct visual connection with the lower space, contains an office, a bathroom, and a lounge that can be transformed into a guest room.

Grober Factory Loft

META Sudio
Barcelona, Spain
© Lluís Carbonell, Aitor Estévez

A sliding stairway, gliding on a rail placed above and along the library, grants access to the upper floor. In this way, the height of the trusses is retained, and building two staircases becomes unnecessary.

121

Use repeating eye-catching details to create a thread throughout different adjacent areas of a space. They can vary in scale, and perhaps even in color, but the design should remain invariable for consistency and coherence.

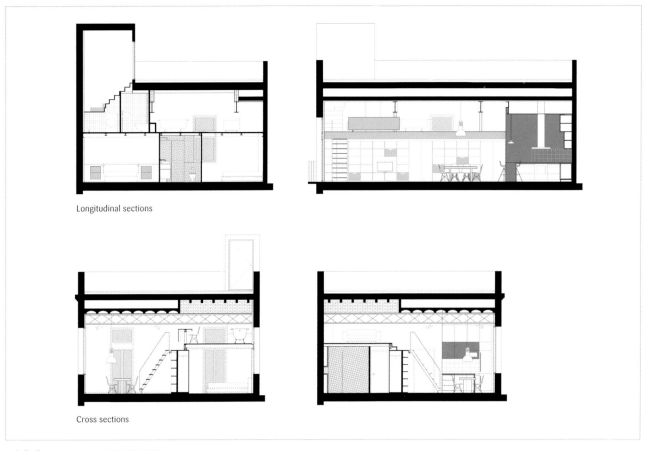

Longitudinal sections

Cross sections

122

Bookshelves can make a
long wall visually interesting.
At the same time, they add
valuable storage space,
avoiding the need for
freestanding bookshelves,
which may interfere with the
open character of a space.

123

Open mezzanines allow for the increase of square footage without changing the perception of a space. As shown in these plans, the lower floor is divided into two rectangular areas, while the mezzanine reveals the square proportions of the loft.

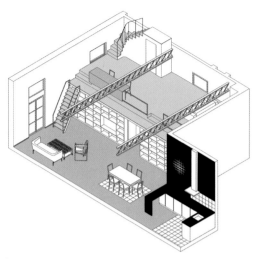

Axonometric view

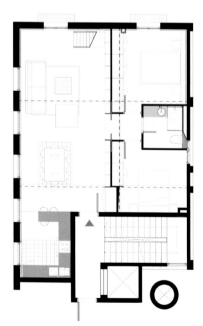

Lower floor plan

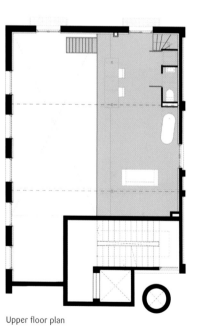

Upper floor plan

124

The headboard is a ingenious decorative solution, allowing for the integration of the electrical installations with the bedside tables and helping to save space.

125

A glass partition between the vanity and the shower over a solid wall creates an open and airy atmosphere in a bathroom. Taking the image above as an example, a wall instead of a glass panel would have cast a shadow over the vanity.

This home/work space belonging to a professional photographer occupies a former industrial building on the east side of Manhattan. Since it must not only serve as his main residence but also host photo sessions, presentations, and other events, huge spatial flexibility is required. To maximize the open-plan layout, storage elements are used to define the different environments.

In tribute to its industrial past, the original tin plates of the 19th-century ceilings have been preserved.

Unfolding Apartment

MKCA // Michael K Chen Architecture

New York, New York, United States

© Alan Tansey

126

Freestanding built-in furniture such as bookshelves can help break up a large open space, while maintaining sight lines connecting different areas. Sliding panels can be used for a complete separation of these areas to satisfy privacy needs.

127

Freestanding built-in furniture can simultaneously serve various areas with different functions. Their multi-functional character makes them an effective space-saving solution.

A former 2,260-square-foot carpenter's workshop is transformed into a garage loft. While keeping its original character, the new space is adapted to accommodate the requirements of its new occupant: room for an electrical sports car and lots of natural light. The front and back walls were the only primary sources of light, providing insufficient natural illumination. To make up for this lack of lighting, an interior courtyard was inserted to bring illumination and ventilation into the middle of the loft.

Carpenter's Workshop

Studio OxL

Van Hasseltraat Arnhem,
The Netherlands

© Irene Van Guin

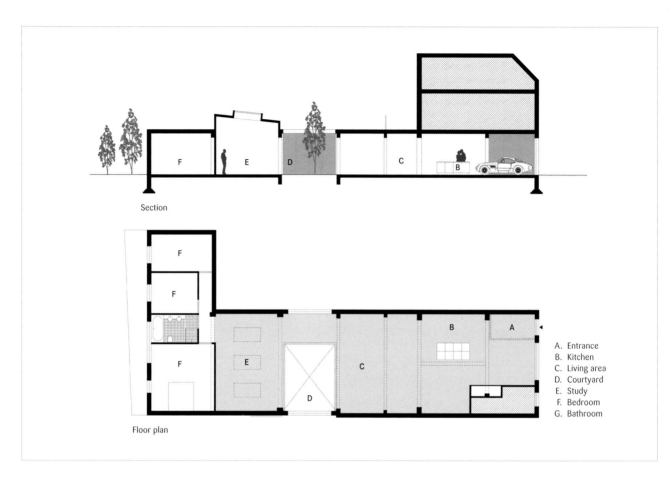

Section

Floor plan

A. Entrance
B. Kitchen
C. Living area
D. Courtyard
E. Study
F. Bedroom
G. Bathroom

128

Interior courtyards with glass walls bring light and ventilation to the spaces surrounding them. They also break a space into different areas while maintaining visual continuity.

The patio divides the loft into two sections: the living areas at the front and the studio and private rooms at the back. With the new layout, both zones receive abundant light.

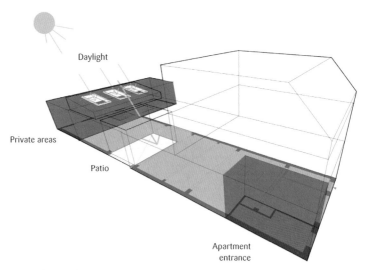

Daylight

Private areas

Patio

Apartment entrance

Volumetric diagram

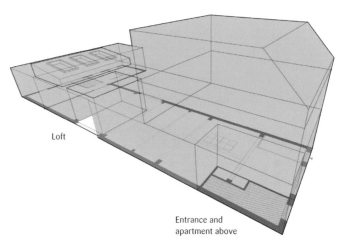

Loft

Entrance and apartment above

Programmatic diagram

129

Interior glass enclosures
allow visual continuity
responding to modern trends
in architecture and interior
design that evolve toward
open environments.

Private Loft

DREIMETA

Berlin, Germany

© Noshe

This loft is located in a landmarked building (at one time a brewery) that features a panoramic rooftop view of Berlin. The couple who own it have created a private and personal retreat amid the city's noise and bustle, filling it with art treasures from around the world. To highlight the art collection, a neutral interior decor was chosen, with relaxing, earth tones combined with an inside layer of brick. The dwelling, distributed over three floors, including the roof and the terrace, includes a guest area.

This room is defined by the balanced elements of wood, textiles, and colors. The furniture has simple lines, and the selected hues, together with the other materials, achieve an atmosphere of serene warmth.

130

Not only does the color white reflect light and helps brighten a space, but also, through a subtle play of light and shadow, it enhances its architectural features.

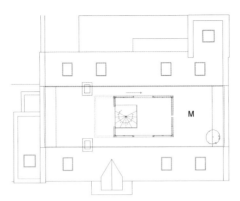

Roof-terrace plan

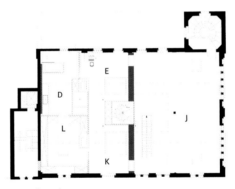

Upper-floor plan

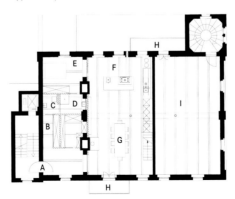

Lower floor plan

A. Entrance
B. Storage
C. Toilet
D. Bathroom
E. Bedroom
F. Kitchen
G. Dining room
H. Balcony
I. Guest apartment
J. Living area
K. Master bedroom
L. Dressing room
M. Roof terrace

131

Spiral staircases are a great way to emphasize the shape of the space that contains them, and make for a spectacular accent. In addition, spiral staircases, with their compact footprint, can significantly safe space.

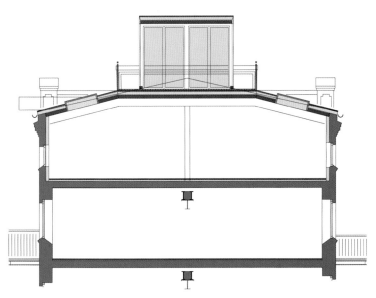

Section

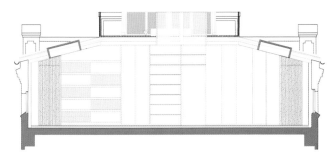

Section through spiral staircase at upper level

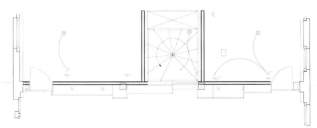

Lighting-plan detail at upper level

On either side of the dining table are benches, which, in addition to seating more diners then chairs could, play against aesthetic expections for a traditional dining room.

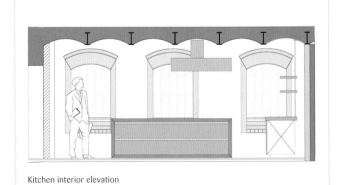

Kitchen interior elevation

For the kitchen and dining area a flooring of cast asphalt has been selected, which gradually over time will develop a unique patina.

In order to highlight the historical nature of the building, it was decided to use materials that were in harmony with its aesthetics. Almost all the dwelling's flooring is made from solid oak.

Located near Union Square in Manhattan, this loft is home to a couple with three children. It has a large number of cabinets that, in addition to performing their storage functions, structure the space, helping to define the different environments. Positioning much of the storage area around the loft's perimeter leaves greater space for the living and play areas for both adults and children. The dwelling has three bedrooms and three bathrooms. On the top floor, a pyramid of glass under the skies of New York houses an office and a multimedia room leading to the terrace.

14th Street Loft

Resolution:
4 Architecture

New York, New York,
United States

© RES4

Since it is located on the top floor, the loft has several glass skylights that brighten up its rooms, without taking space away from the terrace placed above it.

132

Strategically placed,
skylights complement
windows to provide a space
with abundant natural light.
Coming from different
sources, light is uniform,
minimizing uncomfortable
light contrasts.

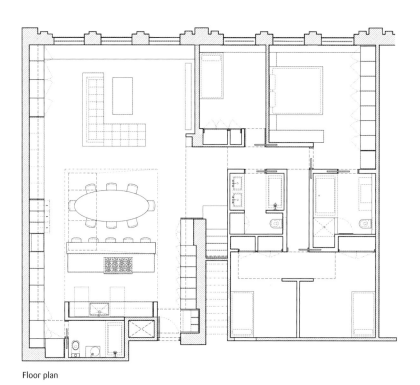

Floor plan

A thick wall of cabinets acts like a
membrane clearly separating public and
private spaces. This design plays in favor
of an efficient layout that concentrates
similar functions in the same area.

133

New homes have adapted to a contemporary lifestyle where the kitchen is just as much of a place for entertaining as a living area. This change often results in the creation of open spaces that allow the cook to interact with other people.

Because the loft has windows only on one side, the design includes various skylights, taking advantage of the loft's location on the top floor of a building.

In the children's rooms, areas for sleeping, studying, and playing are well defined. The furniture is scaled to the size of the children, allowing them to easily reach all their things without the help of an adult.

Family Loft

ZED ZeroEnergy DESIGN

Boston, Massachusetts,
United States

© Eric Roth

A young couple wanting to increase their family acquired this loft, built in the 1990s, and hired the ZED team, who transformed the space, giving it a new, fresh but at the same time functional appearance in an urban environment.

The goal for the living area was to add texture, scale, and usefulness to this new open space. The entrance area has been converted into a lobby with ample storage and a work area that can be used as an additional bedroom. Creating inside windows added light to formerly dark spaces, such as the nursery and guest room.

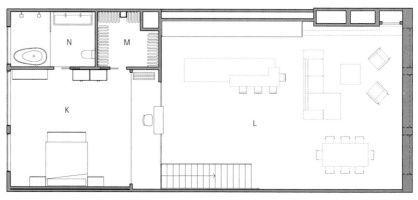

Upper floor plan

Lower floor plan

0 2 4 6 8 10 [ft]

A. Entrance
B. Gues toom
C. Nursery
D. Play space
E. Dining area
F. Living area
G. Kitchen
H. Bathroom
I. Laundry room
J. Office/Mudroom
K. Master bedroom
L. Open to below
M. Walk-in closet
N. Master bathroom

The dark wooden floor was removed, and the cement lying under it was polished, giving it a long-lasting, easy-to-maintain finish, which adds luminosity. Walnut wood, present in many items, imparts warmth and texture.

134

Steel rod or cable guardrails are a strong, lightweight option—compared to laminated glass guardrails—offering unobstructed views, while providing safety around stairs and mezzanines.

135

In lieu of a wall, a glass panel separates the shower from the vanity. The open plan of the bathroom and the wall-mounted vanity give a sense of openness and highlight the continuity of the flooring.

Bond Street Loft

Axis Mundi

New York, New York,
United States

© Durston Saylor

A refurbished loft in a landmark building is the luxury minimalist backdrop for its occupants' art collection of the work of young, emerging artists. One of the goals was to give the 3,400-square-foot dwelling a human scale, organizing the open space into different areas with specific functions and providing it with the commodities necessary for living. Per the client's request, the loft had to offer a variety of seating options for entertaining. With the space layout defined, the finish and color palette are deliberately understated so that the art collection becomes the primary focus.

136

Pieces of low furniture contribute to the creation of a bright and airy space as they highlight the proportions of the room.

137

Warm grays, taupe, and beige tones are safe color choices. Soothing and easy on the eye, one almost never gets tired of them. Against this kind of background, a few choice pops of color can have a dramatic effect.

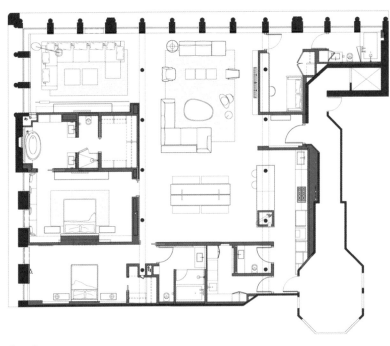

Floor plan

The design gives prominence to a concrete feature wall and stresses the soft gray wide-plank floors with hot-rolled steel detailing. The existing cast-iron columns are highlighted. All these elements lend raw materiality to the space.

138

Loft spaces lend to eclectic décors that give a relaxed vibe to a home. At the same time, the use of colors defines areas in order to bring some structure to the space.

The original columns guide the layout of the loft but are also fully integrated into the design of elements such as the kitchen island.

139

Artwork may be among the
last design decisions in
the decoration of a space,
unless the space is designed
around a particular art piece.
Regardless, the artwork
needs to harmonize with
the space that contains it.

Paschke Danskin Loft

3SIXØ Architecture

Providence, Rhode Island,
United States

© John Horner Photography

This project involved the conversion of an existing loft into a live/work space with two distinct areas for its occupants: an artist specializing in ceramics and light-reflective installations, and her husband, a computer engineer. The design is complete with a series of common spaces such as the entry, a utility room, and a sunroom. The trapezoidal shape of the loft was divided into two architectural themes: cloud and stack.

The opposing themes provide a language for the narrative of two lives—individual, yet intertwined.

Both cloud and stack wander through the effect, negotiating around angles and columns to achieve a unified space. Different themes are expressed through contrasting yet harmonizing materials that support the presence of different but compatible personalities.

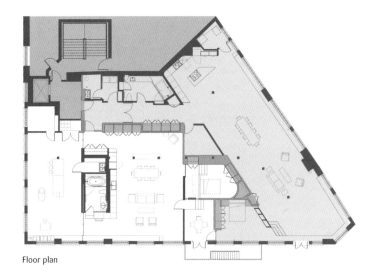

Floor plan

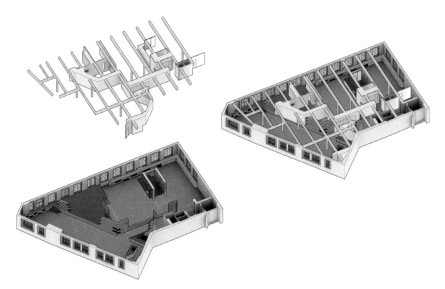

Axonometric views

140

The irregularity of the space and the awkward location of the columns presented a considerable design challenge, but at the same time they opened up new opportunities.

Cloud is expressed through white and translucent materials, while stack boasts wood and MDF casework with steel details. Cloud and stack are mingled throughout the space, but never isolated from one another.

141

Translucent partitions in etched glass or polycarbonate let light through and, at the same time, provide privacy. They also impart a sense of airiness that reminds one of the traditional Shoji screens.

In keeping with the cloud theme, the space flows effortlessly. The effect is heightened by walls lined with continuous low cabinets in contraposition with stone-clad volumes.

The casework acts as the unifying element of the overall design. It is conceived as stacked angular volumes spreading and transforming from closed cabinets to open shelves.

142

Different functions can be
separated by a change in
floor height, avoiding the
construction of walls, while
maintaining the brightness
and openness that generally
characterizes a loft.

143

The character of a
contemporary bathroom
can be enhanced by the
proper use of lighting,
achieving a sharp, fresh,
and serene atmosphere.

Garden Loft

Egue y Seta

Terrassa, Spain

© Vicugo Foto

Once a commercial space, this converted dwelling allows you to breathe nature. Upon entering (through a solid iroko-wood varnished door), you find a garden with local shrub species of varying heights on a pine-bark bed bathed in the light of a false skylight, the antechamber to the house surrounding it. On the left are the public areas: a lounge, excavated from the building's foundations, and, on an upper level, the dining area and kitchen. From there, a concrete walkway leads to the house's more intimate rooms, then a study and living room, and finally a guest bathroom.

Sunken into the concrete foundation of the house, a U-shaped lounge creates a comfortable, yet modern atmosphere that reminds one of the "conversation pits" so popular in residential design from the 1950s through the '70s.

The large stainless steel surfaces contrast with the treated-wood countertops and artisan-brick wall, offering an industrial appearance, at once modern and sophisticated and warm and welcoming

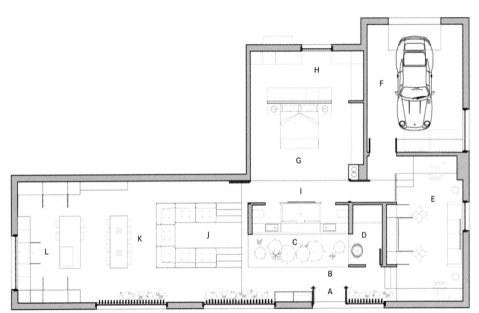

Floor plan

A. Entrance
B. Foyer
C. Interior garden
D. Bathroom
E. Office/Guest
   bedroom
F. Garage
G. Master bedroom
H. Walk-in closet
I. Master bathroom
J. Living area
K. Dining area
L. Kitchen

144

This custom-built headboard made of natural oak and wire mesh stands out for its multifunctional character: it serves as room divider, separating the bedroom and the dressing area, and its back is designed to store shoes.

The shower is the centerpiece of the master bedroom. A formed concrete bench, incorporating the fittings, extends beyond the glass enclosure to become a vanity on either sides of the stall.

Behind a sliding door, and coated with glazed artisan clay, is the guest bathroom. A glass wall allows us to enjoy a garden view while washing our hands.

145

A special room in the house needs equally special furnishings and accessories. Just as a chandelier can catch the eye in a living room, a stylish freestanding washbasin can be the crown jewel of a bathroom.

Twin Loft

CHA : COL

Los Angeles, California,
United States

© Edward Duarte

This project began as a simple enough loft conversion, but
expanded into a twin loft when the client purchased a second,
adjacent space. Not only did the area double, but the scope of
work needed to be revised. The aim was now to differentiate
the two areas so that one could be used as a living space,
and the other for housing guests and/or entertaining. But the
differences had to be subtle enough so that the two spaces
could read as one.

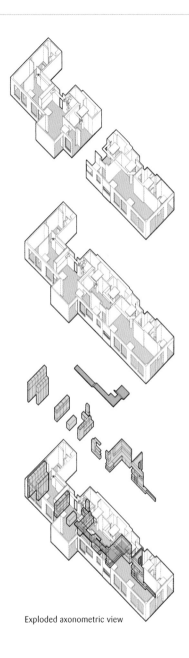

Exploded axonometric view

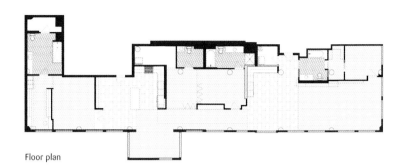

Floor plan

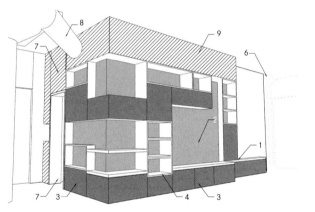

Perspective view of integrated shelf wall

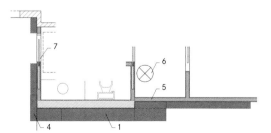

Partial floor plan

1. 2" thick-marble countertop at bench
2. Marble/stone tile veneer
3. Lacquered cabinets
4. Open shelves
5. Wall beyond
6. Existing column
7. New pocket door with stone jamb, threshold surround
8. Existing HVAC duct
9. New drywall to fur and match lacquered cabinets

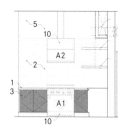

Stove-wall elevation

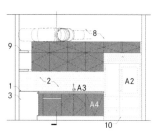

Sink-wall elevation

Island-elevation

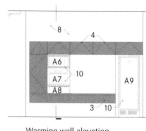

Warming wall elevation

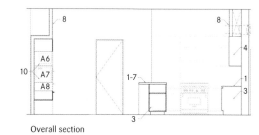

Overall section

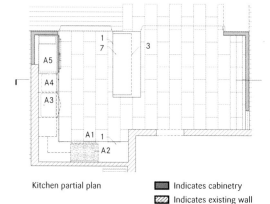

Kitchen partial plan

▨ Indicates cabinetry
▨ Indicates existing wall

1. 2" thick-stone countertop
2. Stone/tile backsplash
3. Under-counter cabinets
4. Overhead cabinets
5. Wall beyond
6. Existing HVAC duct
7. New kitchen island
8. Fur drywall to flush with cabinetry
9. Overhead shelves
10. New appliance

A1. 36" wide Subzero-Wolf gas range
A2. 36" wide Cavaliere euro ductless range hood
A3. 32" wide sink with faucet
A4. 24" wide integrated dishwasher
A5. 48" wide Subzero "PRO 48" refrigerator
A6. 24" wide Subzero microwave with 6" trim panel
A7. 24" wide Subzero wall oven with 6" trim panel
A8. 30" wide Subzero warming oven
A9. 28" wide wine cooler

146

Exposing sprinkler and HVAC systems is a design solution that enhances the industrial—and original—character or a loft. By doing so, it may be possible to lessen the impact on a space's integrity.

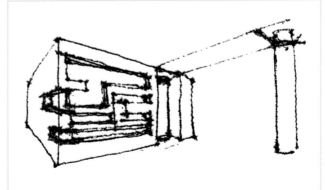

Preliminary design sketch

147

A clear separation between the new and existing elements of a space can satisfy the functional requirements while enhancing the original character of the space.

Loft 78B

Maurizio Costanzi

Rome, Italy

© Maurizio Costanzi

This space, prior to its refurbishment, was neither well organized nor comfortable. But four large windows and a generous ceiling height helped its successful transformation into a bright, spacious, and welcoming home.

With the new open plan, the various ground-floor rooms, including living room, kitchen, and dining room, blend into a seamless whole. An iron staircase leads to the upper part of the building and to a bedroom and study, separated by a glass partition.

Through a translucent glass wall the morning light, entering through the bathroom window, is diffused into the living room.

472 Loft 78B

148

A kitchen island can double as a work area and as an organizer of the space around it. In this case, the island occupies a central position and separates the living and dining areas.

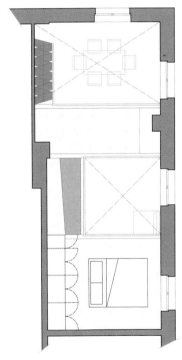

Upper floor plan

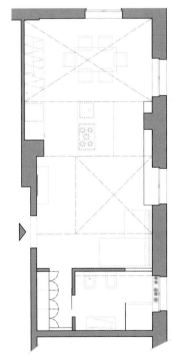

Lower floor plan

474 Loft 78B

149

Polished concrete is a type of continuous flooring material. Because it is highly porous, it is generally sealed with epoxy resin. Over large surfaces, expansion joints are required, but applied in small areas, it can form a continuous surface.

150

A thin-steel-beam/parquet floor assembly supports a mezzanine to maximize the vertical dimension of the space.

DIRECTORY

Architecture in Formation
New York, New York, United States
www.aifny.com

AreaArquitectura.Design
Valencia, Spain
www.areaarquitectura.com

ASZarchitetti
Florence, Milan; Italy
Dubai, United Arabian Emirates
Shanghai, China
www.aszarchitetti.com

Axis Mundi
New York, New York, United States
www.axismundi.com

B² Architecture
Prague, Czech Republic
www.b2architecture.eu

James van der Velden / Bricks Studio
Amsterdam, The Netherlands
www.bricksstudio.nl

Brooks + Scarpa
Los Angeles, California, United States
www.brooksscarpa.com

BRUZKUS BATEK
Berlin, Germany
www.bruzkusbatek.com

Buro Koray Duman
New York, New York, United States
www.burokorayduman.com

CHA : COL
Los Angeles, California, United States
www.chacol.net

DA Architects
Saint Petersburg, Russia
www.da-arch.ru

destilat ARCHITECTURE + DESIGN
Wien, Austria
destilat.at

Diego Revollo
São Paulo, Brazil
www.diegorevollo.com.br

Dreimeta
Augsburg, Germany
www.dreimeta.com

Jaroslav Kašpar / duoton
Prague, Czech Republic
www.duoton.cz

Egue y Seta
Barcelona, Madrid, A Coruña; Spain
Tokyo, Japan
www.egueyseta.com

EHTV Architectes
Brussels, Belgium
www.ehtv-architectes.be

Estudio Teresa Sapey
Madrid, Spain
www.teresasapey.com

Federico Delrosso Architects
Milano, Italy
www.federicodelrosso.com

Gianluca Centurani
Roma, Teramo, Castellazzo Bormida; Italy
www.gianlucacenturani.it

GRADE
New York, New York, United States
www.gradenewyork.com

Ippolito Fleitz Group
Stuttgart, Germany
www.lfgroup.org

Jean Verville
Montreal, Canada
www.jeanverville.com

Jeroen de Nijs BNI
Amsterdam, The Netherlands
www.jeroendenijs.com

Marco Dellatorre
Milan, Italy
www.vemworks.com

Maurizio Costanzi
Rome, Italy
www.mauriziocostanzi.wix.com/architetto